Hard Comes First

Hard Comes First
The Guide to Winning

Rod Ray

Published by Game Changer Publishing

Paperback ISBN: 978-1-963793-44-4
Hardcover ISBN: 978-1-963793-45-1
Digital: ISBN: 978-1-963793-46-8

NOTE: Numbers appearing in superscript, such as [11], indicate a reference or note that provides additional details or commentary relevant to the text. These references can be found in the "References" section at the end of the book.

www.GameChangerPublishing.com

DEDICATION

Dedicated to Merritt, my greatest encourager.
Ashe and Cole, whose incredible courage has made my life rich.
All the great people who have given me permission to be their coach.
The many people with special needs who live boldly.

Hard Comes First

The Guide to Winning

Rod Ray

www.GameChangerPublishing.com

Table of Contents

Introduction

We were created to develop, grow, and live in community with one another. There's no better playground to learn about ourselves and others than college sports. Engrained with the lessons of teamwork, victory, defeat, and sportsmanship, college athletics is a valuable tool that can teach us how to live well.

In *Hard Comes First*, I've combined the best sports lessons with insights gained from having a son with autism. In competitive sports, one team wins, and one team loses. There is no middle ground. The rules are the same for both sides. Both teams prepare, execute, and deliver a result that ends in either triumph or defeat. The raw competition is one of the things we love most about sport. However, life outside of sport isn't supposed to be like this. We become stronger competitors when we understand that winning isn't always black and white.

Coaching players who are in the top one percent of their craft has taught me about toughness, love, passion, and conviction. It is said that a lesson worth learning is a lesson worth sharing, which is why I wrote the book. This book will give you steps and lessons that will help to be rich beyond your dreams. Read, learn, and implement these lessons with conviction and urgency because so many people are counting on you. You'll likely be surprised at how much you gain as well.

CHAPTER 1

There Can't Be a Comeback
if You're Always Ahead

"Mark, stay with us. You're not leaving us today. Darn it, stay with us!"

Mark lay flat on his back in the middle of the tennis court. He had just gone into cardiac arrest. Earlier that morning, he had fought hard in a highly contested battle to earn a terrific win over an excellent player from Armenia, Columbia, who played for UNC Wilmington. We were off to a great start at the NCAA Regional tournament hosted by Duke University. Mark and his teammates were glad to be at the tournament, competing in one of the best NCAA Regionals in the country. It was Wofford's fall break, and the team's spirits were high.

After Mark's win, he had enjoyed a three-hour break, which had included a few laughs with his teammates, a grilled chicken sandwich, and a couple of bottles of water. Then he'd be back on the court, starting another match against a great player from Wake Forest, one of the best programs in the country.

Fifteen minutes into the match, Mark collapsed. He had no pulse or breath. He was dead. The defibrillator's electronic voice echoed, "No pulse, continue shocking." *This isn't happening,* I thought as Mark lay motionless on Court 10 at the Cary Tennis Park, one I'll never forget.

Three fit young men took turns doing chest compressions, trading off as they grew tired. I felt connected to these men as they put all the energy they could dig up into saving Mark. Their only rest came during the short pauses when the defibrillator was used.

The situation looked bleak, and then Mark's eyelids fluttered. Could he still be alive? Was he making the ultimate comeback in front of countless players and fans? We couldn't be sure. Finally, Mark took a natural breath. The crowd of players, coaches, and fans gasped with him. I felt a tear run down my cheek.

I'd seen thousands of tennis matches but had never experienced anything remotely close to this before. The world stood still. I felt like I was in a vacuum. Though surrounded by chattering people, I couldn't hear anything but my thoughts. My mind flashed back to 11 years before, when one of our players, Randall Heffron, tragically died on our campus. He was a wonderful young man, and I had been certain we would lose another.

There's no question that Mark was in the right place at the right time. Numerous caring people dove into action without hesitation. Ryota Nakagi, the Duke trainer who happened to be next to Mark's court in the 30-court facility, didn't hesitate to start CPR. I'll never forget Ryota's poise and professionalism as he took charge. Dr. Mark Zapp was there from Florida to visit his son Logan, who plays for UNC. Mark teaches CPR and was standing next to the court, so he jumped in to help with CPR. And there was T.J., the Duke assistant coach who had lost his father due to sudden heart failure at a young age and who felt his father's presence as he raced to get the defibrillator.

Though normally rivals, these people didn't look the other way or assume someone else would get involved. If they had, this story would have turned out much differently. On this day, there was no rivalry. Everyone had the same goal: to save Mark's life. People from Duke, UNC, Clemson, and Wake Forest surrounded Wofford, and this time, fortunately, everyone won in the biggest match of the year.

The EMS team that got the call is said to be the best in the Raleigh area and has earned the reputation as an emergency room on wheels. When the lead paramedic got involved, he was clearly in charge. You could have heard a feather hit the ground as they rolled Mark's stretcher into the ambulance.

By this point, the area was flooded with first responders, who all seemed to know each other. A police detective approached me and said, "You must be the coach. Get in." And away we went. As we sped to Duke Medical Center, both vehicles flashed their lights, and traffic parted to create a narrow path on the busy expressway.

The tennis community is tight, so the news about Mark traveled fast. From the detective's police car, I received calls from our college president and athletic director. I did my best to update them on what we were up against. It was reassuring to hear their familiar and kind voices, but I remained terrified about what might or might not be happening in the ambulance ahead of us.

I kept thinking about Mark's parents. Mark is from Spain, but Thomas, his dad, was in Madagascar for a tennis tournament with his daughter. I checked the time on my phone and was relieved to learn it was late in Madagascar because I had no idea what I would say to him. I tried to rehearse how that conversation would go. This was not something I had ever practiced. I rationalized that the call would need to wait because it would be senseless to cause alarm when I didn't know more.

I felt unprepared for whatever was going to happen next. As we raced down the interstate at lightning speed, the policeman explained that as long as the ambulance didn't pull over, things were likely going well. I fervently prayed for Mark with both fists clenched as if he were my child. I had prayed for my children before, so I took comfort in knowing that this was something I had experience with.

Once we arrived at the hospital, Mark was rushed behind the emergency room walls. The detective pulled over to the curb, handed me his business card, and told me to call him if he could help. Then he shook my hand, wished me well, and pointed me toward the emergency room entrance. I got out of the car, still in shock and disbelief. I didn't know if Mark was dead or alive, so I didn't want to go inside. But I had no choice.

Stepping inside the emergency room, I surveyed the lobby. Some people were there because their loved one or friend was sick, and they had nowhere else to go. Others were there because of some critical, though non-life-threatening emergency. Then there were those like me, there for someone who had narrowly escaped death or still barely clinging to life.

No matter the situation, we were all scared and uncomfortable; everyone would have rather been somewhere else. Most everyone respectfully avoided eye contact in the emergency room, but I felt a common bond with the people there.

After going through the metal scanner and security check, I signed in with the front desk, hoping to get information about Mark. The receptionist told me to have a seat and wait for my name to be called. I was frantic and couldn't sit still, so I paced the emergency room lobby for what seemed like forever.

An hour later, my name was called, and I was escorted into a large room with dividers that gave a semblance of privacy but not too much. This was essentially a stabilizing and evaluation area for the people who had come into the emergency room from ambulances. The place was hectic and bustling. Mark lay on a gurney, hooked up to monitors tracking his heart rate, blood pressure, oxygen saturation, respiration, and temperature. I guessed these numbers had dramatically improved in the last hour, but I didn't know.

I sighed with relief when I saw that he was awake and mumbling. He knew he was in the hospital, but that was it. His left eye was swollen, partially shut and black, but he seemed glad to see me. As we talked about what had happened, Mark was in disbelief. He remembered nothing about the incident, which had taken place only two hours earlier. He had lots of questions. He remembered winning the morning match and starting his second match, but that was it. I didn't know what this lack of memory meant for him, but it frightened me. A few hours later, he got a room on the hospital's cardiac floor.

Coaching friends from Duke, Gardner Webb, UNC, and USC took care of our team at the tournament while I sat with Mark at the hospital. The other coaches were terrific. They helped our players with food, transportation, and motivation. Many of them continued to call me for days after Mark's incident, and I appreciated it. Their kindness taught me the importance of reaching out to people. I now never assume someone is too busy to receive a call of encouragement and kindness.

Once Mark was stable, I called his father, Thomas. He had been trying to reach Mark but had assumed that either something was wrong with his phone or, like most twenty-year-olds, he was too preoccupied to answer or return the call. By the time I reached Thomas, my explanation was well rehearsed. Explaining to a father who is six thousand miles away that his son nearly died but now seemed okay was difficult but important. Thomas trusted me when his son left home before his freshman year, and I felt his trust on the phone. He didn't know it then, but he gave me a gift of confidence and human kindness at one of the most vulnerable moments of my life. I handed my phone to Mark, who spoke to his father in Spanish. I don't speak the language, but I could tell their conversation was a loving one.

After the tournament, the team went home to Wofford without me. I stayed for eight more days until Tomas and Mark's sister arrived, and the medical team was ready to perform surgery. Those eight days in the hospital had a huge impact on me. I slowed down, and things I hadn't thought about in a long time became incredibly important. Being present and showing up for someone took on new meaning. Coaching friends continued to call me, and I appreciated it more than I ever thought I would.

When someone makes a play that goes beyond what we think is possible, we'll often call it a miracle. Now, though, I describe them as good fortune. I'm convinced that what happened to Mark was a true miracle. The medical team said that he had beaten insurmountable odds by making it to the hospital alive. I don't believe that Mark's story happened by chance. Too many good things occurred for me to write it off as merely good luck.

Mark is a fantastic player. As a freshman, he was All-Conference in doubles and was on the first-team All-Freshman team. Mark's ability to thrive under pressure is one of the things that makes him great. Despite his situation, he remained poised and in great spirits. He kept his sense of humor and was nice to everyone in the hospital. We cried together once and laughed together a lot. I was in awe of his ability to go with the flow. The roles had reversed. Mark was the teacher, and I was his student.

Before Mark returned to school for classes, his teammates came to the hospital to see him. This was an essential time for them, as they were grieving over Mark's loss. The bond between teammates is unlike so many others. Teammates don't have to be alike to love one another. These teammates loved one another, and Mark had made a considerable impact on them and was a vital part of the team. His humor and playfulness often brought people together, and this was one of those moments when we needed that.

The Duke cardiac team was terrific. I'll never forget his surgeon's coaching session with Mark two days before the surgery. Dr. Sun is a world-renowned cardiac electrophysiologist. He explained to Mark that he wasn't confident about Mark's tennis future but could say with certainty that Mark's life would be incredible. He explained how Mark would see the world differently in the future, and the impact he would make would be powerful.

After Dr. Sun left, I wondered, *How will I make an impact?* Telling Mark I would be right back, I got up and ran down the hall to find Dr. Sun. "Excuse me, sir," I told him. "That was the best coaching I've ever heard."

I thought, *Inspiring others to live a remarkable life. Could this be the best coaching ever? Is this the whole purpose of coaching? Are sports really a mechanism to be used to make the world a better place for everyone?*

I won't forget the eight days I spent with Mark in the hospital. My wife was completely supportive and encouraging, telling me that if it were one of our children, she'd be so grateful to the coach who stayed. She demonstrated her empathy for others during difficult situations. We had a home to care for, bills to pay, a dog to feed, and exercise in rain or shine. All the normal stuff continued to pile up, but she never missed a beat in encouraging me to be the person I wanted and needed to be. Sometimes, we need to do what's right, whether it's convenient or not. This was one of those times.

Wofford was also incredibly supportive. Our athletic director never questioned my decision to stay, and our players had excellent practices without me. Many of them stepped into leadership roles and kept the team moving forward in preparation for the next tournament and the spring season.

Mark's situation has been challenging. His dreams have been shattered, and he's still facing many uncertainties and fears, such as what his life will entail moving forward. However, I'm beginning to see good things, too. For example, Mark works as a tutor for children in an after-school program in one of the poorest areas in town. I've seen the smiles on those kids' faces when they say goodbye to Mark as he leaves. I'm catching small glimpses of what might be in store for him. Often, something great can come down the pipeline after a hard experience. I'm counting on that pipeline, and you can too. The next time we are dealt something hard, let's take the stance that hard always comes first.

There's no guarantee that something great is coming, but there's a better chance when we're accustomed to looking for it. For example, since Mark's experience, I've learned to hug players like never before because we never know where they might be in the future or what might come next for them.

This book may change how you see adversity because you'll be on the lookout for future opportunities. Believe it. There's evidence to prove it. I'm sharing my story because I've been in places where I felt helpless or, even worse, hopeless. But I learned a way out. This is what I want to share with you.

CHAPTER 2

The White Jesus

I have friends whose children died young. I don't claim to know what that is like, but I do know how terrible it is to mourn a child. I'm keenly aware that the parents of special needs children grieve in profound ways that can be painfully hard to explain. It is difficult not to think about what could have been. The grief centers on the loss of how you thought your life with your child would be.

I also know that our lives can sometimes take on new meaning. A shift can occur from wanting a life that aspires to achieve everything to one that desires to help other people. We can change to see the world from a uniquely beautiful vantage point. Compassion and empathy for those who are hurt can become stronger than ever before. With all the pain that comes with it, hurt can become a blessing if we take a leap of faith and not let it define us.

The first time I learned about autism, I was sitting in a movie theater, watching *Rain Man*, starring Tom Cruise and Dustin Hoffman. Autism is a spectrum disorder because it encompasses a wide range of challenges. The movie was my only reference to the disorder, so when I learned of my son's diagnosis, I had no idea what it meant for him and our family. All I could think about was what I had learned from the two-hour movie. There's a saying, "If you've met one person with autism, you've met one person with autism." This has certainly been my experience. My journey with autism is unique in many ways, but I've learned some things that are worth sharing. It isn't just the events per se; seeing them more empathetically is what's most important.

Bill Porter is a Hall of Fame coach who holds the record for the most state championships of any high school tennis team in South Carolina. I coached Bill's kids for years, yet there's no question that I learned more from him than they did from me. Most of what I learned from Bill had more to do with being a good person than with tennis. I knew Bill's teams played hard for him because they liked him.

Bill wasn't just a coach; he also worked with special needs kids at Irmo High School. He had a blast with the kids on his team and in his class. I'm not sure if it was legal, but Bill used to take his special needs kids fishing with him on his boat. When Bill retired from coaching, he started a successful landscaping company. Bill drove 30 miles each day to pick up one of the students who used to be in his special needs class, a kid named Scott. He also gave Scott a job in his business. Bill taught him how to use the heavy equipment and gave Scott a purpose when no one else ever thought about him.

One day, Bill and his wife Kim decided to move to Charleston to live near their two adult children and their children. Bill turned his business over to his brother with one condition: he had to keep Scott as an employee and pick him up every day. This Hall of Fame coach went out of his way to make a kid with special needs feel like a million bucks. Bill did not act like he was doing any favors; instead, he was the lucky one. Being a Hall of Fame coach is about finding joy in doing more for others than yourself. Strategy and organization matter, but the real Hall of Fame is the lasting and compelling execution of investing in others.

The Porter family is fantastic; they are the type of people who make you feel better just by being in their presence. We all know these types of people who enjoy others without passing judgment. They are excellent listeners. They're sincerely interested in others because their opinion of themselves is neither too high nor too low. It is hard to pinpoint what else makes some people this way, but it must have something to do with how they care for others, are comfortable in their skin, and have a sense of peace about them. Another way to put this is that they live in harmony with the world.

When Bill and Kim left Columbia and moved to Charleston, they purchased a home in an inner-city neighborhood near the river. Bill is an avid fisherman who, ironically, doesn't eat fish. So, after a big day of fishing, he began the tradition of parking his truck on the street corner and handing out packages of the catch of the day to people in the neighborhood. When Bill's truck is on the corner, folks know it is time to get free fresh fish. Bill's gesture of feeding the community earned him the nickname "White Jesus." People line up to see what White Jesus has brought.

Bill happily distributes the fish, as there is always more than enough to share. He feeds many people, and although it isn't quite the "feeding of the five thousand" depicted in all four Gospels, it seems pretty darn close. He treats his customers well, learning their names, shaking their hands, thanking them for coming, and expecting nothing in return. He enjoys having the opportunity to be nice—nothing more, nothing less.

I can't help but think about the nickname "White Jesus." Black people gave it to him. I think most of us have some biases when it comes to how we see things. The nickname White Jesus suggests that the "white" part was significant to this community. If this assumption is correct, kindness could be exponentially more remarkable when we act generously and hospitably towards people who don't look or act like us.

A few months after earning his new nickname, Bill tragically lost a young grandson in a car accident near his home. As you might imagine, this was a terrible event. The family was devastated. This was one of those deaths that are hard to understand or explain because there was no reasonable explanation.

This accident was even more complicated because the driver was a family member. Upon learning of the accident, I called the great coach and told him that this was the time for his best coaching and that he would be the one to teach his family about forgiveness and love. Bill and many others in their family had already done this. I started that call thinking that I would teach them and coach the family about forgiveness. But as I hung up the phone, I couldn't help but realize that I had a lot of forgiving that I needed to do. Otherwise, my anger and disappointment at how people had treated my son would eat at me in ways I'd never survive. I didn't know how to start, but I knew it needed to happen and hoped that one day, my heart would be healed by a shower of forgiveness toward others.

Those close to the family asked themselves why such a bad thing would happen to such loving people. Grief from death can differ significantly in older people, who have lived an entire life, and young people, whose story doesn't seem complete. When children die, dreams of shared experiences die with them, so the grief continues and can be all-consuming. The same is true when any dream dies, but it is magnified when the dreams that we have for a child die.

The funeral was moving. The people of Bill's inner-city neighborhood showed up in large numbers. In a time when America was angry and confused about race and politics, people of all races not only expressed shared grief but also brought food and flowers. Thoughtful people of different ages and socio-economic backgrounds mourned together. Race was unimportant, but humanity mattered immensely. Hatred was absent. Plain and simple, everyone grieved for a child who had died too young. Empathy is a powerful emotion.

In the best-selling book *Emotional Intelligence*, author Daniel Goleman says empathy is understanding another's emotions. He describes the three types of empathy as cognitive empathy, the ability to understand another's perspective; emotional empathy, the ability to feel what another person feels; and empathic concern, the ability to sense what someone needs from you.[1]

Understanding what someone needs helps them, and I can't help but believe that Goleman is correct in noting that action is also an essential part of empathy: turning caring into doing. This is precisely what the people in Bill's inner-city neighborhood did. By doing so, they made Bill's family and themselves feel better.

Funerals are strange ceremonies. They're designed to help us grieve, note the significance of the person's life, and help us move on. When an older person dies, we sometimes call the funeral a celebration of life. And to be honest, most people feel this way. We think this way when our grandparents die at a ripe old age. However, when a child dies, celebrating doesn't seem right. Many people believe in heaven or some other afterlife, and we can be comforted when we believe we'll see our loved one there. But it is still hard to make sense of the death of a child.

The grief felt by Bill's family did not end with the funeral, so Bill went to work, converting his garage into a bike shop. I don't think he had read Goleman's *Emotional Intelligence,* but he had a lifetime of experience of reading people and taking action. He needed healing, and so did his family. So, he began collecting beat-up old bicycles and fixing them for kids in the neighborhood.

It didn't take much time before word got out, and folks started dropping off bikes at Bill's house. Bill had a collection like you have never seen. He took old bikes and added new tires, seats, handlebars, and paint. He had every type of bike you could imagine: racing bikes with numbers, little bikes with flowers painted for young girls, bikes with banana seats, cruisers, and bikes with bells on the handlebars. You name it, he had a bike designed to fit every kid's dream and desire, regardless of age.

One day, right before Christmas, Bill delivered close to a hundred bikes to the local community center. A parade of children was there to receive their first bikes as Bill and his new neighborhood friends and family handed them out. The run-down community center was filled with joy, laughter, and the best type of disbelief, which can only come from a happy child.

Bill is more than a legend; he's a hero. He has a new calling that's more important than winning championships. He still grieves the loss of that beautiful child, and I'm guessing that pain will never go away, but he's also doing so much good. He's creating smiles and making people happy. The White Jesus is warming hearts on the coast of South Carolina. He has a spirit that can live on forever. Sometimes, the only way to survive is to help others. When I go to Bill's house, autism does not matter; I like it there a lot. Kindness solves many problems.

Suffering is essential to personal growth. We tend to focus on ourselves, but the remedy is to get busy helping others. Coach Porter demonstrated this to me in the worst of circumstances. Autism has allowed me to execute what I learned. We all have our worst-case scenarios; let's be sure to perform when the next opportunity shows up.

CHAPTER 3

No Struggle, No Story

When most of us see incredibly successful people, we rarely see the obstacles they had to overcome. The same is true when we see top collegiate athletes.

Watching so many young people go from struggling to excellence has impacted how I see people. We are amazing when we overcome difficult circumstances. We're not amazing just because we were born that way. What makes us special is how we do neat, surprising, and difficult things.

College athletes grow because they are pushed to overcome difficulty; however, only a very low percentage of people reach their full athletic potential in college. There is always room for improvement in even the best college athletes' careers. Some professional athletes reach their potential, but this isn't even common for professionals.

A 2023 report by ESPN listed the top North American athletes of the last century.[2] The top five were Michael Jordan, Babe Ruth, Muhammad Ali, Jim Brown, and Wayne Gretzky. As good as these players were, we can all agree that they were people, and people have people stuff, which includes struggles. The struggles we encounter play a vital role in molding who we become. This is true for us just as it is for the top five athletes of the last century, so it is vitally important that we understand that not all struggles or limitations are bad.

Becoming a college athlete takes a lot of sacrifice. A recent study by the NCAA reports that only approximately two percent of American high school students go on to play Division I college sports.[3] Those who do are typically goal-oriented, driven, and used to overcoming obstacles. Division I athletes are one level below professionals.

College tennis is more of a bridge to the pros than ever before. The Intercollegiate Tennis Association recently wrote an article stating, "Today, we celebrate some new heights achieved by former student-athletes in the April 4th ATP/WTA Rankings. Altogether, seven former collegiate athletes now rank within the Top-Ten of the Singles and Doubles ATP and WTA Rankings, showing just how valuable college experience is on tour."[4]

Since tennis is an international sport, most professional players don't grow up dreaming of playing in college like an American high school basketball or football player does. Instead, their sights are set on turning pro early on. Their goal is to win what's known as a Grand Slam, which is winning the four top tournaments in the world in a single year. To tennis players, winning a Grand Slam is the same as winning the Super Bowl or World Cup.

A study by MarketWatch indicates that roughly 3.5 percent of college athletes are international. That number is disproportionately higher in some sports, such as tennis, which is above 30 percent, and for Division I, it is even higher.[5] The international scope of college tennis has undoubtedly played a hand in raising the level to where it is, so close to the elite professional level that the average sports fan cannot tell the difference.

Another factor that has recently boosted the level of college tennis is COVID-19. Many lower-level tournaments were eliminated during the pandemic, making college tennis a more viable option and pathway to the pros. Since prospects from around the world are competing for spots, earning a position on a Division 1 team is challenging. As elite as college tennis is, reaching one's potential in college is almost unobtainable. This is because athletes often don't reach their prime until after college, when many have moved on to careers outside of their playing careers.

Experienced coaches agree that coaches rarely miss on talent during the recruiting process. The evaluation process for recruits is tireless, but coaches understand athletic characteristics such as hand-eye explosiveness, mobility, footspeed, size, and strength. More time and energy are put into evaluating the athlete's heart. Mistakes are much more prevalent when forecasting a player's drive, commitment, and determination level. Most college athletes' level of success is determined by qualities other than talent.

To attain their highest possible level, athletes need an abundance of perseverance because it takes so long for most to reach their prime. For example, in distance running, male athletes are believed to hit their peak around 27.[6] In tennis, where movement is based on sudden starts and stops, the prime age is also thought to be in the late 20s. However, recent evidence shows that this age is increasing as players take advantage of growing opportunities to take better care of themselves. This data shows that players likely don't reach their prime until five years after college. Therefore, college players chase a ceiling they'll never reach unless they play professionally after they graduate.

This raises the question of the most accurate way to define "great." As a coach who spends hundreds of hours a year in the player development space, I hesitate to describe someone as great who isn't attacking their potential. In other words, I find it more exciting to see passionate people pursuing their best than someone relying only on ability.

The high achiever typically has a combination of passion and ability channeled in the right direction. However, people can change, and greatness can be attained by someone who once underachieved. My job is to discover why someone isn't pursuing greatness and help them achieve it. It might be that they're scared to go after something and fail. If this is the case, it isn't that they don't want excellence; instead, they've been programmed to believe that failure is bad. Igniting self-belief in someone's life is an incredible opportunity, one that should be embraced when it appears.

Assessing greatness is an interesting process. Should greatness be measured as how successful people are compared to others? Or can someone be great compared to what common sense believes they will accomplish? A sound definition of greatness measures the degree of our overachievement compared to our perceived ability level.

For example, are you great if you're seven feet tall and can dunk a basketball? This seems like an easy task for someone this tall. How about someone who's five foot six inches tall and can dunk? Indeed, this person should be considered great. This is true in every field. Hence, an argument can be made that a wheelchair tennis player might be great or elite, while a non-disabled player who defeats the wheelchair player is only average.

We can agree that this is what coaches and teachers should believe, but what about managers and employers? How about friends and neighbors? Where do we draw the line? Are we only supposed to lift people when compensation is involved?

Everyone runs their own race, even when part of a college team. They come from different backgrounds, families, and situations and face their own set of challenges and opportunities. They might be on the same team and share the same goals, but their race is their own, unique to them. This is true not only in college sports but in life. Once we learn this, life gets cleaner. Much of the mess and confusion disappears when we learn to stay in our lane and do our best with what's in front of us.

Our team once had a fantastic athlete named Parks Thompson, who should be labeled great, considering his start in life. Parks came to us because his college recruiting process had taken a left turn due to a prolonged stress fracture in his back. As a young player, he had attended a strong tennis academy with a tradition of sending many players to top colleges. The injury and the delay in the recruiting process had led Parks to take a gap year before beginning college.

Although overcoming a stress fracture in the back is no small task, this is not what sets Parks apart. He was born with a clubfoot, which was initially ruled inoperable. In *Podiatry Today*, Dr. A. Douglas Spitalny, DPM, writes about his over 30 years of treating patients born with clubfoot disability: "Many of us who treat clubfeet in children and teenagers rarely see these kids progress to sports, let alone enter the military."[7] Clubfoot is not uncommon, but it usually makes high-level sports difficult.

Parks benefited from parents who wouldn't accept no as their final answer. Doctors initially told them that any athletics involving running were off the table. Fortunately for Parks, his parents did not take the advice of the first three doctors they visited. Eventually, they traveled across state lines to find one willing to operate. After many surgeries and lengthy rehabs, his club foot was corrected. Slowly, Parks learned to walk, run, and play sports, including tennis.

The example of perseverance was established. In Park's teenage years, when he had the stress fracture, he had already overcome so much that he saw it as a temporary delay rather than a permanent obstacle. His struggle with his clubfoot, under his parents' guidance, made the struggle with his back more manageable. He knew about adversity. He also knew what it was like to focus on the cards in his hand rather than compare his accomplishments to those of other children his age.

When Parks came to Wofford, he had a motor that made him fast. Speed is essential in tennis, and explosive speed became Parks's dominant weapon as a Division I tennis player. Speed and footwork are non-negotiable for great tennis players. Players move so fast that college players typically wear holes in their shoes within three to four weeks due to sliding several feet over pavement after connecting with the ball. This young man, who had been told he wouldn't run, became the fastest player on a team of athletes explosive enough to slide on pavement. In other words, Parks was the fastest in a group of high-speed people.

Parks's smile was brilliant, and his sleek build and swagger made him appear like a young, athletic Mick Jagger on the cover of *GQ*. It is hard to imagine what Parks and his family went through when he was young. It is also hard to understand how he must have felt as he began to develop into an incredible athlete with blazing speed.

It's no coincidence that Parks is a visionary entrepreneur who helps others grow their businesses today. From an early age, he developed the skill and attitude to see beyond the impossible and turn dreams into reality. He is sharp-witted and possesses an energy that lights up a room. However, I can't help but wonder if he would be the man he is today if it hadn't been for his struggle. The evidence is clear. There's a high probability that his struggle is a large part of what makes him great. Parks's story is undoubtedly one of someone attaining greatness.

As we endure discomfort, very few people ask themselves if the struggle is a gift. It is usually only when the struggle is gone that we recognize that it might have been used for good in our lives or the lives of others. One of the most widely read spiritual writers in recent years, Henri Nouwen, writes, "The gifts of life are often hidden in the places that hurt the most."(4) This statement leads us to believe that challenge is one of the most significant components of being human. Challenges often lead to insight, personality, empathy, and honor. When we look at hardship as a benefit, we can see our challenges as the pathway to a richer life.

I recently attended the most beautiful wedding for a former player. Many of his teammates attended, and we had a great time together. During the ceremony, the wedding official spoke about unconditional love. At the time of the wedding, I was in a bad place because I felt betrayed by people I cared about. This feeling caused me to have anger in my heart. I realized that my love towards these people had become conditional based on their behavior. I was treating the relationship as transactional: If you do something for me, I'll do something for you.

The anger and sense of betrayal allowed me to grow and better understand how love is supposed to work. Love isn't supposed to be transactional. Upon reflection, I understood I needed to go through the storm to become the person I wanted to be. I didn't even know this level of love existed before.

I wouldn't want someone I care about to spend their life with someone who has never been dealt a difficult hand or faced adversity. Difficulty is where the story of courage and passion intersect to write a great story. If there's no struggle, there's no story. This is true in sports, history, business, and relationships. Allowing students and children to fail is one of the best gifts we can give them so their stories can be beautifully written.

Everyone deserves to have people who unequivocally believe in them. When we bet on people and believe in them, we don't see failure as final. Good things happen that far surpass winning and losing when we genuinely bet on another person with all our hearts. Having an unwavering belief in others is what coaching is about. I often tell my players they are welcome to use my faith in them until they find their own.

People can do so much more than is often expected. Some people saw a club foot, while Park's parents saw possibilities. Finding ways to believe in others is necessary for a winning attitude, and being optimistic about the success of others is an excellent way to live. Parks is fortunate because he had the benefit of being born into a family with loving parents who were used to winning. What if this hadn't been the case? When I recognized this about

Parks, I began to understand that there are unlimited opportunities to help people who aren't in my family.

Taking care of our families is a given responsibility. Getting outside ourselves and helping others is what leads to a richer life. In college sports, we see this when players put their team's needs over their own. This is one of the great benefits of college sports that we need to study and be leery of losing. We need to acknowledge the victories others are having and look for ways to lift them above ourselves. Though counterintuitive, such an approach will change our life's mission.

CHAPTER 4

Comparison is the Thief of Joy

I conducted an experiment with dog owners that seemed to work well. The outcome should have been obvious to me without testing, but the test was conclusive. All you need to do to make a dog owner happy is tell them their dog is the best-looking dog you've ever seen. When you praise random pets, you'll be amazed at the smiles you'll receive from their owners. I've witnessed a marked positive change in the owners' body language, and they instantly assume that I'm brilliant and have a skilled eye for recognizing beauty and greatness.

Some pet owners receive many compliments, but others do not. The owners who receive many compliments generally respond differently than those whose dogs don't draw much positive attention. For example, my dog, Lexi, is a tightly wired German Shepherd. People typically react by stepping back when they see her. My friend has a Golden Doodle. People often want to hug Golden Doodles because they are inherently cute. The last time someone said my five-year-old German Shepherd was adorable was when she was eight weeks old.

The American Kennel Club describes German Shepherds as courageous, confident, and smart, but they need supervision when playing with other dogs. Many of the best players I've coached share similar character traits. Both the Golden Doodle and the German Shepherd need love and attention; German Shepherds don't look like they need it. Why would anyone think a GoldenDoodle needs or deserves more love than a German Shepherd? All players need attention, not just those who are the easiest to coach.

Compliments and praise are potent tools for gaining influence and persuasion, but that shouldn't be their point if we're sincere. I think the point should be kindness. Some children get very little praise compared to other children. Our comments can give some children an unconscious advantage that we don't even realize we're giving them. When we compliment people who don't usually receive much recognition, the compliment can have an exponential impact. The compliment is a good deed for the giver, and the impression it makes on the receiver might be more remarkable than otherwise because it catches them off guard.

I've noticed some people receive more than their share of compliments while others may go years without receiving any. I think most of us accept this fact of life without paying it much notice. However, reaching out to complement marginalized people can have a huge positive impact. Everyone desires approval from others, but the marginalized typically feel disapproval and disdain more than they do acceptance. I learned from coaching that compliments are much more effective than constantly correcting or putting someone down. And from autism, I've learned that ignoring people isn't good, either.

College campuses are a testing ground for acceptance. Students long for approval and are often willing to go to any lengths to get it. We want our students to feel accepted and loved just as they are. I love my players and have high standards for them. My love for them is unconditional and not dependent upon results. It is given to them no matter if they win or lose. Many people don't receive or accept this type of unconditional love. They learn that love is conditional and dependent upon how they perform, look, and act. This behavior can be carried into their adult lives, influencing who they choose as friends and how they spend their time, energy, and resources. The need to fit in can take control of a person's life if they aren't careful.

The need to fit in is one of the reasons so many in America are overextended with credit card debt. The Motley Fool recently found that Americans had $841 billion in credit card debt. A report by CBS estimates that the average household has $9,990 in credit card debt per household.[8] Living beyond our means can signify that we succumb to a desire to fit in even when we can't afford it. No one wants to be like this, yet the need to fit in is so strong that we feel like we can't help it.

On the surface, fitting in reassures us that everything is okay because we have approval and feel like we belong, but this feeling is temporary until the next purchase is made. What we need is acceptance without fitting in. There's power in being an individual.

Think about how the desire to own trendy products works. According to a recent study by PricewaterhouseCoopers, more than half of consumers use search engines to gain information for purchases.[9] Often, consumers search for something because they've seen other people using it, giving it credibility. This is certainly true for material possessions such as cars, houses, or clothes, but the things that most deeply capture our hearts are often more intangible, such as attaining something we've worked towards or are invested in, like education or a skill. At the highest level, the things we adore most are our children and families. There's a reason that we know better than to cross a momma bear. They are known to be highly protective of their young.

Just like other college students, college athletes possess a desire for approval. They have spent years honing their craft, so their sport often becomes a huge part of who they are. The sport is usually woven deeply into their being, and what they do often creeps into becoming who they are. It becomes hard to separate the two. These players often seek support and encouragement from fans, coaches, and peers, but that doesn't mean they get enough. In their purest form, sports are supposed to be fun, but when we make them more than a game, they can become an unhealthy part of our identity. This makes it hard for many players to put down their sport when they're finished.

College athletes' desire for approval can come from a false sense of performance-based confidence. However, steadfast belief in oneself doesn't come from outside sources; confidence comes from within. We're told that fine clothes and expensive cars give us confidence, and research shows that material things can boost short-term confidence. However, lasting confidence comes from qualities such as integrity, truthfulness, kindness, and perseverance. We want to learn these things from sports and life so they can shape us into more interesting people.

Strong players come in many different shapes and sizes. They don't have to have the same characteristics, but they all need confidence. However, confidence isn't an easy or automatic mindset for most athletes. When asked what players want to improve the most, their number one choice is overwhelmingly the mental game. This comes from putting in hard work on the physical and technical sides, but it also includes doing the work on the inside so a player isn't hampered by judgment or fear.

Sometimes, players must become better losers before they can become better winners. This doesn't mean they must enjoy losing or become less competitive. Instead, they must lose the fear of failing to play more freely. The same is true of life outside of athletics. Being scared of life can lead you to miss out on enjoying it. When my son received his autism diagnosis, I was so focused on his challenges that I missed out on seeing some of his strengths. My fear got in the way of my joy.

For long-term success, character development is essential. This is one reason teamwork is often a big part of player development. Teamwork is undervalued in American society, but it plays an incredible part in determining who we are.

Most college players don't accomplish the goals they once dreamed about without pain and suffering. Most of the time, players don't become the stars they thought they would; many don't make the starting lineups, and only a few win championships because the level of competition is so much higher than they realized. A false sense of greatness often comes from being a big fish in the smaller pond of high school or youth sports.

However, the best learning and personal development lies between heartaches, disappointments, and goals that don't quite come true. Within these valleys, people feel stuck and overwhelmed by a lack of confidence. This place of turmoil is where growth takes place, giving us one more reason to embrace the struggle in sports and life. We often feel lonely and isolated when we're struggling, and athletes are no exception. Sport, like life, is supposed to be challenging because the point of it is personal growth.

The high points are sky-high for college athletes, while the low points can dip extremely low. Our society glamorizes college athletes when they win and villainizes them when they lose. Everything about college athletes is publicized, from the team GPA to the latest signed recruit. This gives athletes valuable experience in dealing with disappointments. If they embrace these experiences as educational, they can make themselves stronger when handling life's tough moments.

This toughness is one of the reasons employers often seek out college athletes. Student-athletes are used to facing setbacks and returning to work without wasting time, making them more valuable in the workforce. To be good team players, athletes must learn to communicate with their teammates when down, low in confidence, and lonely. Being able to do this well builds trust in others and themselves.

Dr. Vivek H. Murthy, 19th and 21st surgeon general of the United States, tells us that loneliness is our country's number one health concern. In a letter, he states, "People began to tell me that they felt isolated, invisible, and insignificant."[10] College athletes are susceptible to the same feeling of loneliness, and their emotions are often heightened due to the intensity of their highs and lows.

The insatiable desire for significance cannot be cured by sport or achievement. We can't get enough approval or likes from social media to fix our need for belonging. We long to be known and appreciated as individuals who have value. The U.S. Surgeon General's *Advisory on the Healing Effects of Social Connection and Community* provides a glossary to aid us in understanding our current state. This glossary includes definitions such as:

- **Belonging** – A fundamental human need, the feeling of deep connection with social groups, physical places, and individual collective experiences.

- **Collective Efficacy** – The willingness of community members to act on behalf of the common good of the group or community.

- **Loneliness** – A subjective distressing experience that results from perceived isolation or inadequate meaningful connections, where inadequate refers to the discrepancy or unmet need between an individual's preferred and actual experience.

- **Norms of Reciprocity** – A sense of reciprocal obligation that is not only a transactional mutual benefit but a generalized one; by treating others well, we anticipate that we will be well treated.

The advisory goes on to state that approximately half of U.S. adults report experiencing loneliness, with some of the highest rates among young adults.

The U.S. is widely recognized as the wealthiest nation in the world, so we should ask ourselves why feelings of loneliness and isolation run so high throughout our country. The answer isn't clear, but there are things that we should recognize. Church attendance is trending downward among major religions, including Protestant Christianity, Catholicism, and Judaism. More people live alone due to changes in family norms. Dr. Murthy states that our rapid pace of life, leading to less social connection and purpose in our busyness, has contributed to our loneliness.

Individuals in the autism community spend an inordinate amount of time alone. A study reported by *Neuroscience News* found:

> Rates of loneliness are substantially higher among autistic compared with non-autistic individuals. This observation refutes the persistent stereotype that autistic individuals are not motivated to seek meaningful social relationships. More plausibly, social environments systematically exclude people with higher levels of sensory differences, impeding opportunities for autistic individuals to form meaningful relationships.[11]

This study predicts that people with autism are four times lonelier than people without. Addressing loneliness for all people is important, but the risks in the autism community are substantially higher. Because people with autism already have high levels of anxiety in social situations, they risk a great deal when entering a social situation.

When athletes pursue their goals, they understand that they're taking a chance at not reaching their goals. People on the autism spectrum are often in uncharted waters, too. Understanding this with an eye toward empathy is essential to increasing autism awareness. When it comes to sports, players know there's risk involved in competing and training hard—including the risk of giving it your all and still not measuring up. There's also the risk of getting injured. The effect of injuries often goes far beyond the physical setback because emotional trouble will usually outlast physical recovery.

High-performance college coaches are emotionally engaged with their players. There's hardly a day in the year that I don't think about each player on our team by 10 a.m. The passion and singular focus injected into having a good team is intense. The hours are unconventionally long. It is a high-stress job that relies on the top-level performance of young people, who are often conflicted and distracted with where they fit in the world.

College coaches aspire to get to know their players well in a short period. By the time four years are up, coaches know each player's dreams, where their identity lies, and what keeps them up at night. This level of depth doesn't happen in the typical work environment where people come to work, do a job, and go home.

The four years of college as a student-athlete are set in an intense space where time is compacted because the team trains, studies, travels, and lives together. Time on a college team exists in a vacuum, unlike any other time in the student-athlete's life. Hence, their experiences with each other are turbocharged. The years after college are much different because people's living arrangements, as well as their interests and hobbies, are more diversified.

In most cases, it takes ten years of year-round play for someone to become an expert tennis player. These years are full of setbacks. The skill of navigating difficulty is precisely why players matriculate and become successful in life. Winning in tennis is rarely just about talent alone. It takes abundant skills and toughness that can only come with perseverance.

Exceptional players are typically ultra-competitive, so setbacks are more challenging to them than they are for most people. This means developing the ability to charge back from disappointment is critical for them. If a player has an extreme amount of natural athletic ability, some of their development may be temporarily delayed by the lessons that failure teaches. No one has so much ability that they escape the pain of growth. Since responding to adversity is a skill, those forced to learn it early have an advantage in the long term. This is why we should see failure as an opportunity for long-term growth rather than a short-term problem.

Injuries can play a significant role in the maturation and development of athletes because they create a time of emotional turmoil that generates inner conflict and doubt. Injured players can become depressed and lonely when they don't possess the emotional tools to cope appropriately with the stress and disappointment of missed playing time. They can often experience a loss of identity and disappointment from the loss of accolades they were counting on receiving from the years of sacrifice. No one wants injuries, but we shouldn't fear them because good things may be on the other side of the growth they can cause.

The investment principle of "buy low, sell high" is easy in theory but difficult in real life because our emotions get in the way. The same is true in our personal lives. Prudent behavior is to quit being emotional and lead with the discipline of betting on ourselves when our value appears low. There's a lot of upside when you do this. It's best to believe that hard comes first and the best opportunities arise when you persevere through hard times. The low point is where champions go all in on themselves and others.

Anyone can have faith when life is going great. Commit to buying in on people, including yourself, when the circumstances are hard-hitting, and you'll reap unimaginable rewards. With hard work and discipline, you can learn to buy in when the market is low for yourself and others. If you don't have this habit, it is time to start because no one was created to be a victim. God creates his kids to be winners, but hard circumstances often come first.

Injuries can be confusing and cause significant setbacks for players. Coaches need to understand how emotionally strong the injured player is and if they are ready for the challenge. The coach also needs to know if the player possesses the toolset to help them get through it. For example, do they understand how vitally important their attitude is? Do they know that bodies heal differently, so a doctor's opinion might be off by a few weeks or months? How will they handle the uncertainty? Rehabilitation is often physically and emotionally tricky before the recovery is complete. Some college players have always been on top of the food chain, so this could be their first athletic setback, requiring a level of patience they have never needed.

With the proper support, setbacks can equip us to better deal with problems we will face later in life. We must understand that whatever we're going through might prepare us for something better. Disappointments can train us to handle more significant issues with grace and courage. Our attitude before, during, and after facing frustration will determine whether we move forward stronger and wiser or become emotionally torn.

Disappointments such as job loss, injury, lack of playing time, or problems with our children are all situations of strife that we can learn to get better at dealing with. The challenge's intensity level might differ, but the steps of the process are the same. Focusing on what we control and not projecting or comparing are critical to happiness and fulfillment. Life doesn't get easier. It typically gets more complicated, but we can improve our skills in dealing with tough times. Every tough time is an experience for us to learn from. Trusting that our path is our path and that comparison is the thief of joy is crucial.

CHAPTER 5

David Never Saw Himself as the Underdog

College sports in the U.S. are extremely popular. A recent report by the NCAA reports that Division I athletics generated nearly 16 billion dollars in revenue the year before the pandemic.[12] No other country in the world does college sports even close to how the U.S. does them.

At Wofford College, the facilities and support for student-athletes are outstanding. The student-athletes have an incredible experience competing at a high level, developing into great players, and making lifelong friends. Our fields and courts are beautiful. The team stays in nice hotels on the road. We have a strong coaching staff and committed support personnel. I can't imagine why anyone would need more.

However, athletic departments like ours don't have the same amenities as the "Power Five" schools possess. However, this isn't necessarily a disadvantage. For example, learning that you can never give in to accepting an excuse or, even worse, creating one of your own is an advantage. We're lean compared to our larger competitors, so if we plan on winning, we can't miss a trick.

In many ways, we're no different from the local coffee shop that wins customers and thrives, even though Starbucks is on the same block. Success in this mode is about hustle and creativity. Being small can teach you how to hustle. If you don't learn to hustle, you'll miss out on countless opportunities in life. We've all seen large and gifted athletes who waste their talents because they only rely on their size and genetic strength. What starts as an advantage often leads to a disadvantage in the long term.

The story of David vs. Goliath is one of the most popular to come out of the most-sold book in the history of the world, the Bible, which, according to the *Guinness Book of World Records*, has sold more than five billion copies.[13] Yet the story has one central confusing point: David was never the underdog.

The scene begins with a stalemate between the Israelite army, led by King Saul, and the Philistines and their mighty warrior, Goliath. At six foot nine, Goliath is a giant everyone in Saul's army is afraid to face. He calls to Saul's army for 40 days, asking them to send a worthy adversary to meet him in single combat. David, a shepherd boy, goes to King Saul and convinces him to let him fight Goliath. He tells King Saul how he's used his sling to kill lions to protect his sheep and that he's confident that he can do the same to Goliath.

Since Saul is out of options, he gives in and allows David to fight the giant, but not before attempting to persuade David to take his armor with him into battle. David refuses the armor and instead goes into action with a sling and five smooth stones.

Picking out one of the stones, the young shepherd slides it into the sling and twirls it above his head at high speed. Before Goliath can act, David slings the stone into the giant's forehand and kills him. As the Philistines watch in shock, David stands over Goliath and cuts off his head using the giant's sword. Praised as a hero by Saul and the Israelites, David gives all the credit to his God.

The most potent part of this story is that David never saw himself as the underdog. David's belief was much bigger than the giant he faced. His mission statement directed him to believe that he couldn't be stopped. If he had made an apples-to-apples comparison of himself with Goliath, the battle would have been over before it started, but he didn't make that mistake. He entered the competition from a position of strength rather than a position of fear.

The sidelines were filled with people the world would have believed were more equipped to fight the giant than David, but they were scared. "Underdog" isn't a term that compares or looks for strengths. It only tells part of the story. We want the whole story to include possibilities rather than just half-truths.

Mariam's Dictionary defines an underdog as "a loser or predicted loser in a struggle or contest."[14] The term originates from 19th-century dog fights where the loser lay on the ground beneath the winner, the top dog. This is a desperately grim picture of defeat. As a competitor, the underdog is thought to have little chance of winning a fight or contest—someone with little status in society.

The crux of the matter rests on how vital the issue at stake is to you. For example, it is one thing to be the underdog in a negotiation you don't care much about, but an entirely different matter when you have worked for something in business or sport. In this case, there can be pressure as you battle for something where the odds are stacked against your success.

The real question is, when you are in such a situation, can you keep your wits about yourself and not overreact to the pressure being applied? I often have the opportunity to practice this tactic in my work, and I'm confident it has improved me. But what about when you care so much that you would be willing to give your life for success? How about when it is your child? Can you remain calm and see the world calmly and clearly? In my case, the underdog mentality was now personal beyond my work.

I believe that everyone has advantages and disadvantages. This mindset gives me creative energy and resolve to find and execute the best version of myself. The idea of the underdog is based on the concept of comparison, which we've already established is unhealthy. Saul's soldiers who stayed on the sidelines were caught comparing. They couldn't see their strengths. They likely had more ability than David, but it wasn't about ability because they let their fear take over.

In Malcolm Gladwell's best-selling *David and Goliath: Underdogs, Misfits, and the Art of Battling Giants*, he explains how weakness creates innovation.[15] For example, David was innovative in combat and did not fight conventionally. Attacking from a distance without armor was an advantage, but Gladwell doesn't address one of the most crucial parts of the story: David didn't see himself as the underdog because he had God on his side. David was incredibly optimistic throughout the entire process of slaying Goliath. It could be said that he was the original "glass-half-full man."

We once had a talented player on our team who struggled with negativity. Whenever something didn't go perfectly, he would immediately complain that everything was wrong. Most of his teammates weren't like this. They were better at handling uncertainty, so they were generally better able to ride out storms. He and I had countless conversations trying to uncover and discover his troubles.

One afternoon, we were leaving the courts after a physically and mentally tiring practice, and he looked at me and said, "How do you expect me to be positive when everything is going so badly?" At some time or another, I believe most of us can relate to this question, but not David. He wasn't afraid to fight the giant because he knew what he was supposed to do.

Most of us have played the role of a dark horse. I love this phrase and believe in the power of being a dark horse with all of my heart. I've never liked the term "underdog." Dark Horse vs. Underdog? What's the difference? The difference is so profound that you should learn it and never forget it.

David could be described as a dark horse but never an underdog. A dark horse rises from an unknown position to achieve strength or success that no one thought they had. They show ability, intelligence, fight, and resilience that no one knew about. A dark horse is an unexpected winner. The term comes from horse racing and refers to a winning horse that the gamblers didn't expect. On the other hand, an underdog begins at a disadvantage and stays at that same level of disadvantage throughout the challenge they face.

Here's an important lesson: never let someone tell you that you're an underdog. You might be a dark horse because they haven't heard of you or your strength yet, but if you keep the right mindset, they just might. All you need is a chance and the courage to allow your strengths to shine, but if your mindset isn't right, it will be hard to overcome a bad attitude.

Like many teams, we train ourselves to be positive. We have practices and standards that help us focus on the positive, such as making a gratitude list daily. This tool is a starting point, but there's so much more to it. Living a life of abundance instead of scarcity exemplifies a positive mindset. It isn't about what you have or don't have but what you do with your gifts.

We all know negative people who are grateful for their "stuff." The problem is that the "stuff" doesn't do it. Saul's soldiers had equipment, but David had a greater purpose. This set David apart from the many trained soldiers on the sideline. Establishing your purpose is an essential step to getting your mindset right.

David used the skills that he had developed to protect sheep from wild animals, but his biggest weapon was courage and confidence from his faith that he had God on his side. David's slinging skills were finely tuned, so he was ready to battle. This gave him self-assurance, but he possessed more than just skill.

Picture David selecting five smooth stones to take to battle. What kind of David do you see? As he bent down to choose the five stones, did he think, *Oh, shoot, what have I gotten myself into? This is a terrible idea. There's been a mistake. Can someone tell Saul to send another guy?*

This isn't the David I'm picturing. I see David demonstrating excellent body language, like a future Hall of Fame quarterback confidently approaching the line to lead his team. The David I see is like Michael Jordan, Kobe Bryant, or Lebron James, who, when the game is on the line, says, "Give me the ball." David's focus is like Novak Djokovic's as he approaches the baseline to serve out the match on the most significant stage in tennis.

David didn't view himself as weak. He faced the giant intending to win and wasn't faking his courage. This is what great athletes do. They bet on themselves to win even when the critics find reasons they should lose. In 1 Samuel 17, David first had to believe that he would kill Goliath. Next, he convinced Saul that he was the right man to take down the giant. If David hadn't been entirely convinced that he would win, Saul wouldn't have accepted the risk of betting on the shepherd.

We can't expect others to bet on us if we aren't willing to bet on ourselves. None of Saul's other soldiers were willing to put themselves on the line. They had the right equipment, were trained, and were older, but they still didn't have what David had.

The difference was that David knew his greater purpose, had faith, and believed in himself. He wasn't afraid to lose. We need players who aren't afraid to fail. When you believe, you play faster, stronger, and smarter. I must be convinced a play will work when I tell players to run it. A coach who doesn't believe in their players does more harm than good. The same is true of parents, bosses, spouses, and friends.

When asking a player to run a certain play, I sometimes say, "Run play [X]. If it works, you get all of the credit. If it doesn't, I'll take all the blame because I know it will work." The play isn't the most critical part. What's most important is the execution, which comes from conviction. A good coach injects confidence. A great player has belief.

The story of David and Goliath took place three thousand years ago. Although King Saul was a large man with armor, he failed to trust God. The young shepherd, David, did not miss his opportunity. This is why his story remains one of the most powerful stories ever. Many critics try to twist it into being the story of an underdog. That isn't the case. If David were alive today, I'm one hundred percent certain he'd tell us he was never the underdog.

This story is in the Bible because we can have David-like experiences when we know our calling and purpose. We're supposed to get this part right. This usually means saying no to many things to get one thing straight. When you know your purpose, your mindset changes, and mindset is what separates winners from losers.

I recently asked a young athlete if he was a spiritual man. Why would I ask him this? What does it have to do with tennis? The reason is simple: if he possesses the same level of belief that David has and is willing to take the bet, he will be a darn good player. If he doubts his purpose and who he is, he might still be a good player, but he's not likely to be as fearless as he could be.

I want a player who believes he's on Earth for a purpose, that his life isn't an accident. Someone who feels loved and understands that the results of a tennis match don't determine their life's worth. Such a player will get closer to reaching their potential than one who doesn't know why they're here. College is an excellent place for players to question, wrestle, and grow into their identity.

Believing you are loved beyond measure doesn't create weakness but strength. David knew this, and we need it, too. Once that concept is grasped, the ability to play fearlessly grows exponentially. A player might win because they have more talent than their opponent. What I'm talking about allows a player with less talent to win. Helping such players to win is what coaching is all about.

Tests are essential to the growth of faith. Trusting in something we can't see is a challenge for an athlete who has trained hard to overcome obstacles. We often need a test that we can't work our way out of to grow into who we are capable of being.

We won't live life to its fullest without substantial testing requiring the development of courage. Some people face more challenges than others, but everyone faces hard times. Those who seem to have it easier are often less skilled in dealing with difficulty than people who face challenges more often. Parents hurt their children by spoiling them. They need to allow their children to experience a healthy amount of failure so they can develop courage. The next time you face something challenging, remember that this test might just be what you need to get to another level.

Challenges are relevant to how we perceive them. Some people will say that life is hard, while others would trade their left hand to have that person's challenges. For example, I recently helped a young man with autism apply for a job. As I helped him rehearse his script, edit his PowerPoint, and practice entering the room, I couldn't help but think how courageous he was. People with autism have this in common with the great athletes on my team.

Once again, by being the teacher of a man with autism, I learned a lesson about bravery that will help my Division I athletes. He taught me about being a tough-minded person who competes daily and rises to the challenge. "Per aspera ad astra" is a Roman Stoic phrase that means "through hardship to the stars." Just as athletes can learn from brave people such as Navy SEALs and firefighters, they can learn how people with disabilities execute under pressure. Sometimes, this bravery is demonstrated just by walking through the door. You can't be in the best rooms with the best views if you don't gather the courage to climb the tallest stairs.

If given the choice, most of us would prefer the most straightforward path with the least resistance. We see this as technology improves our living standards each year. We can't wait to get the latest and greatest gadget to make something easier than it was before. A wealthy society has a way of providing more shortcuts each year. Although the new technology is helpful most of the time, it doesn't always benefit us in the long run. For example, electronic communication is excellent, but it makes having a difficult conversation easier than face-to-face in the short run. However, by not having difficult conversations in person, we might miss out on learning some of the conflict-resolution skills gained from challenging moments.

One could argue that college freshmen should ask to be provided with experiences that teach them how to hustle instead of being the recipient of unearned awards. "We need experiences where we face giants, so don't you dare make it easy for us" should be the uppermost goal of every educational experience for the people we care about.

Hard comes first. Great never precedes hard. It always succeeds it. Joy is different from happiness because joy is what we feel when our emotions are brought out, and our feelings are catapulted beyond what we expected. Something better than we could have imagined is described as joy. Coming from despair into happiness can often be described as joy. We need pain to appreciate joy, so pain can, indeed, be good.

People who haven't faced difficulty still experience happiness but not at the same level as those who have overcome challenges. Difficult times help us improve and add meaning to our lives, so we should consider them an advantage. Hence, the parent who allows their child to fail better equips that child for the future than the parent who is ultra-protective. Permitting your child's failure when you have the ability and means to protect them is a gift that takes maturity and a true sense of purpose to execute. It would benefit our communities and country if this mindset were taught and embraced in parenting classes.

The struggle is the connective tissue that creates the toughness, stamina, and muscle required to win rigorous battles. When young athletes have early success, they often receive it without putting in the work needed to win later when the competition is fiercer and more numerous. This can create frustration and burnout later, so focusing on what we're learning rather than short-term outcomes is essential. A pattern of overcoming difficulty is a teacher worth hiring.

Experience teaches us to trust that what we learn in difficult times will add insight or value to our lives that we would otherwise not acquire. Marcus Aurelius's famous saying, "What stands in the way becomes the way," has stood the test of time as a tried and true Stoic philosophy. It is easy to understand that those things blocking us are the keys to another level, but only if we remember this during and after difficulty.

In *Man's Search for Meaning*, Viktor Frankl, a Jewish prisoner, writes from a Nazi concentration camp, "When we are no longer able to change a situation, we are challenged to change ourselves."[16] People are generally averse to change, so changing ourselves is incredibly difficult unless we are forced to do it. This is why difficulty is so good for us. We typically resist change unless we're completely out of viable options.

This was the case for Frankl in the concentration camp. Although humiliated, starved, and treated terribly in unimaginable ways, he still had the choice to change on the inside. If he failed to change, he understood that he would be destined to die a miserable death.

Frankl, a psychiatrist and neurologist, created a type of therapy called logotherapy while working with suicidal patients. The Greek word "logos" means purpose, plan, meaning, and divine reasoning, while "therapy" means healing. His idea is that everyone needs meaning to live their best life.

Much of Frankl's book comes from his experiences in the Auschwitz concentration camp, yet people today continue to search for meaning in the pursuit of the good life. If this were true, wouldn't everyone who achieved a "good life" be happy? Knowing this isn't true, that there isn't a correlation between achieving a good life and being fulfilled, is worth noting and, at the least, examining and questioning where we should put our energy.

Logotherapy aims to connect spirit or human will to health so the patient desires life. Frankl developed some of his logotherapy before being sent to Auschwitz, but he added much to it in the concentration camp. It is noteworthy that the therapy he used to help his suicidal patients was the same process that more than likely saved his own life. Of the 1.3 million people taken to Auschwitz, 85 percent, or 1.1 million, didn't survive.

In logotherapy, the therapist focuses on the spirit and the basic needs of humanity. The spirit is often blocked due to trauma or illness. Frankl believed that he had to survive to write his book, which would be helpful to so many people. He learned so much in the concentration camp that he was determined to live to finish his book.

In the concentration camp, nothing external was within the prisoners' control. They were continuously confronted with the worst situations imaginable. The only thing they had power over was their internal response. Victor Frankl was in the concentration camp for nearly four years, during which there was often little or no hope of ever getting out, yet he learned that he had to stay present and focus on the future.

Frankl learned to continue loving his wife even though he had no proof that he would see her. He remained hopeful even in the direst conditions. To Frankl, this was a choice. Later, even when he learned that she had been killed, he continued to love her. He notes that this is love in its purest form. While suffering, he realized that life was worth living.

In sports, we hear of athletes getting burned out. Other times, they will quit their sport to focus on academics. Paradoxically, their grades often drop after they do. So, did they stop athletics to focus on academics or tire of failing to meet expectations and losing? When our team's GPA is typically much higher than that of the average student, I can't help but think that academic interest isn't the reason for quitting. It seems more likely that the case is similar to what Frankl noticed in the concentration camp. Losing becomes too painful, and they give up. I've rarely seen a winning player burn out.

Being tired of losing is a common mantra in sports. Sometimes, players can work harder to do something about it; occasionally, a coach makes a trade, and other times, players find inner resolve. Investors often sell when they are losing. Buying low and selling high is hard to execute because our emotions take over. Like disciplined investing, great athletes buy low and sell high. Never sell when "your market is low." There is almost always opportunity when the market is low, but not when melancholy creeps into your soul. Theoretically, we understand this about markets, but what matters more is that we know this about our personal growth.

Viktor Frankl learned that when we can't change our outside circumstances, we are forced to change our mindset. This is precisely why knowing the difference between failure and opportunity is essential. With over 14 million copies sold, *Man's Search for Meaning* was not written for entertainment like many best-selling books. It was written to provide insight gained in the laboratory of one of the worst places in history. Frankl believes his point is clear. Life can have meaning in the worst circumstances, even in the horrendous concentration camps of Nazi- Germany.

In sports, we also learn that we are better competitors and more productive when we let go of those things outside our control, shifting our effort to improve things within our control, such as mindset, perception, and attitude. An athlete who acquires this skill through early failure will grow stronger. This reemphasizes how critical failure is, especially when done in the context of learning opportunities. For example, I just got off the phone with one of my players who lost in the finals of a money tournament. After speaking with him, I'm confident he learned more from the loss than he would have if he had won. This situation was a win-win because we celebrated him making the finals while still recognizing that there are always things to improve when pursuing excellence. Athletics is not a zero-sum game.

In recent years, many of us have had the opportunity to practice letting go as we dealt with the disappointments and frustrations that came with COVID-19. Ironically, the act of surrendering is an act of power. It allows us to shift our attention to things within our control, making us more effective. It is almost impossible for an athlete to reach their potential without these skills.

An argument could be made that our players are overwhelmingly successful after college because of the type of people attracted to a solid academic school like ours, but I believe there's more to it. It makes sense that they are forced to grow because we don't make it easy for our student-athletes. They aren't given easy classes or special tutoring. It is actually more difficult for them than the average student, yet their grades are consistently strong. Learning to adapt and compete academically and athletically helps them succeed 10 or 20 years later when life becomes taxing.

College isn't supposed to be the highlight of an athlete's life. Instead, it should be part of their education process. If this is true, no one honestly believes spoiling athletes is in their best interest. The struggle is an enormously important part of the student athlete's education. We shouldn't look for ways to make it easier for them. Years later, they will benefit if they have developed strength from distressing experiences they can draw upon.

There is currently talk of how college athletes should be treated as employees. However, being an employee has a much different purpose and goal than pursuing an education. When we think of college sports as a job more than an education, we devalue the benefit of sports as a serious component of education. Looking at it this way, we have shifted our belief to one in which the value is more significant for the fan than the athlete.

This just isn't true. Few things teach character on every level better than sports. For example, sports teach us how vital losing is. We've all seen those parents who protect their children from losing by giving them everything they can in youth sports. This isn't wise because losing is crucial to human development. Does anyone think having the best tutors, clothes, and equipment improves the quality of real life in the long run? A spoiled prince will not make a great king.

We're not supposed to try to fix everything. I haven't been able to cure autism. However, I've learned that there is a lot in me that I can improve. Knowing what to fix, what to love, and what to leave alone is vital if you want to be impactful and happy. I'm betting you have something you need to love more and fix less. I learned that I wasn't supposed to change autism and what needed to change was me.

CHAPTER 6

The Four Truths of Growth

When parents pray that their child will be born healthy, they often add secret requests. These pleas are driven by fears and hopes that can be subtle. The success we hope for our children is derived from personal experiences that form biases. All biases can prohibit growth because no one reaches their potential when they have preset ideas. This revelation has helped to develop **The Four Truths of Growth**. If you're going to make it to the land of rich living, you've got to encounter and embrace The Four Truths of Growth:

1. Our unmet potential is the most significant tax we will ever pay.

This really speaks to the idea that when we don't tap into our full capabilities, it costs us—big time. Think of it like this: every bit of talent or skill we don't develop, every goal we shy away from, ends up being a missed opportunity. It's like paying a tax on what could have been. This is why focusing on self-development is so crucial. It's about not leaving what we could achieve on the table. So, by pushing ourselves to grow and make the most of our abilities, we're not just improving—we're also avoiding that hefty price tag of unfulfilled potential.

2. Nobody is just that way, especially me or you.

It does not pay to be critical of others or ourselves. At the same time, we need to understand that no one is "just that way." Good coaches help people to grow and develop. They see the best of possibilities in others. Everyone can see others the way that developmental coaches see people because everyone can grow and change beyond what we think is possible.

3. Talent is not the issue, so do not allow that to be an excuse.

The best talent doesn't always win, and lesser talent doesn't always lose. Never allow a lack of talent to be your reason for checking out. Willpower and work ethic almost always have a ceiling that we haven't reached. This is a better area to focus on than talent level. Work as if you have no talent. Play as if you're the most talented person in the world.

4. Obstacles are challenges for winners and excuses for losers.

This is a fundamental difference in mindset between those who achieve success and those who fall short. Some individuals have a tendency to make excuses when faced with difficulties, while others view the same obstacles as opportunities to excel and grow. It's important to recognize that both winning and losing are habits formed by our responses to challenges. To prevent falling into a pattern of making excuses for setbacks, it's crucial to cultivate a mindset of hunger and optimism. When you encounter an obstacle, instead of seeing it as a barrier, treat it as a chance to develop and strengthen yourself. This approach not only builds resilience but also turns potential setbacks into stepping stones for success.

CHAPTER 7

The Best Competitors

Those of us without a disability take so much for granted. Spending time around people with built-in challenges helps us understand that we often underappreciate our current situation. I've learned a lot from having a child with autism. These insights are worth sharing because they provide awareness, leading to empathy that can create action to help people. Helping people in a way that is not transactional is one of the most important things we can do.

There are many different sources of stress, and some people have more than others. That being said, the burden of stress is significant for parents of those with special needs children. The University of Wisconsin did a study on families' stress levels when there's a child with special needs, and they found it comparable to the stress level of soldiers in combat.[17] I want to clarify that I have the highest respect and admiration for our military and its people, so when I read the study, my first thought was that people who have never been in war have no idea what it must be like. It does bring light to the fact that the stress levels of the mothers are also incredibly high.

The worry and what-if scenarios in the minds of combat soldiers must be overwhelming. This is easy to comprehend when considering the danger, fear, uncertainty, and discomfort they undergo. And if the study is correct in comparing stress hormones, it gives us a deeper understanding of what families of special needs children deal with in a way that makes sense. This study seems unbelievable, but I get it. What makes it hard is that these parents are walking around Main Street, U.S.A., without support while trying to mix in with everyday people.

When a country is at war, the families at home often tie a yellow ribbon around a tree to symbolize the distance between themselves and their loved ones. This symbol is used to unite families who share this experience. The community respects the family as they appreciate the difficulty and stress that the family must feel. Families with special needs children often feel left out and alone. The loneliness from the isolation of a world that's moving forward doesn't go away, and these families don't get a yellow ribbon.

Having a child with autism is challenging but can also be gratifying. I have so much respect for my son and others with challenges. One of the benefits I've received from my son's autism is that I've gotten to know more courageous people with challenges than I would have otherwise. When I meet someone with a disability, I see someone who is brave, fearless, and strong. I'm more empathetic than I would naturally be. Empathy towards others helps take the focus off the things that might otherwise feel like burdens.

We can learn a lot from people with disabilities because much of their success is due to the little things that typically go unnoticed. This is how everyone succeeds. Do the little things better, and good things will come. The little things they accomplish add to considerable accomplishments that continue to go unnoticed most of the time. We can learn from their willpower.

My son's autism has given me a gift for seeing the world differently and learning from a changed perspective. Anyone who has worked with special needs kids will testify that the parents of children with disabilities share the common denominator of courage. I refer to my friends with children on the autism spectrum as being in a club. Like an old American Express advertising campaign stated, "Membership has its privileges."

There's much to learn about preparing for competition from people with disabilities. They often have tremendous courage. They have backbone, toughness, and grit. They do not want pity. They want to win. It is important to note that life gives us different definitions of winning. Finding the true purpose and meaning of winning is super important. This is how our dictionary defines winning: "To achieve victory in a contest or fight." If this is the correct definition, there's no doubt about the respect we should give to people with disability challenges. They've flat-out earned it.

Lisa Lane, an attorney by education, has spent most of her career as the director of Project Hope Center for Autism in South Carolina. As a mother of a young boy with autism, she made serving families with autistic children her vocation. In an interview with *Today*, Lisa said, "An autism diagnosis will change every aspect of your life, from how you relate to religion to how you select your salad dressing. You can lose yourself in autism but also find yourself."[18] This is precisely what happens to people who serve others, especially those who help people with disabilities. I believe the same can happen to anyone focused on helping others. I see this in coaching: when you believe in your players, you want to inject that belief into them for their benefit.

I tell my players that tennis is what they do; it isn't who they are. They have to know their purpose, which isn't tennis. Tennis might open doors for them and shape them, but it isn't who they are. People with autism are the same way. There's an interesting distinction between someone saying that a person is autistic and saying that they have autism. They have autism, but it isn't who they are. Who they are is a beloved child of God, just like the tennis players on our team.

Loving someone with autism takes life to another level. It is a spiritual rather than worldly type of love, one you enjoy knowing that the person will not do something for you in return for the love you give. This is an unusually fantastic type of love. This is love in the correct form—no expectation of attention, accolades, or celebrations, just simply taking care of God's kids.

Disabilities are common. The CDC now states that 26 percent of Americans have some form of disability.[19] This means that millions in America care for people with disabilities, and millions of people with disabilities are not receiving personal care or attention from a loved one because they don't have one, or their people are either incapable of helping or consumed with their own problems. This represents a gap that can be changed, especially when we consider the opportunity to love others without expecting anything in return.

According to the CDC, a disability is any condition of the body or mind (impairment) that makes it more difficult for the person with the need to do certain activities (activity limitation) and interact with the world around them (participation restrictions). This broad definition implies that most people either have a disability or are close to someone who does.

I feel much different about autism today than I did 15 years ago. This transformation originated from surrendering my fears and understanding that I cannot control everything. I never knew that letting go creates power while holding on takes it away. Autism brought my family into a new game without clear rules. I was forced into letting go, which has helped me in other parts of my life.

Learning that my son Cole had autism was a moment I was not ready for, but so much has changed for the good since then. I've met great people I would have never met and learned to see the world differently. I understand when people pray for babies to be born in good health. I think it is fair to assume that good health is what we desire for our children, friends, and family, but I can't help but wonder if that prayer is actually on point because we don't know what good might come from the challenges. This is all part of learning to let go of the reins so I can be free to live life on its terms and not be afraid of what may or may never happen.

If we believe in a bigger plan, we're not privileged to know what good might come in the future or even what's best. It is best to pray that God's will be done instead of for more self-rewarding outcomes. Some circumstances or events that we think are bad at the time are later proven to be good. We're not privy to what will happen in the future, so the thing to do is what the best competitors know: be where your feet are and don't worry about the future.

Things might be bad at the time, but that doesn't mean they will always be bad. Jesus wants us to know this, so he told his disciples, *"In this world, there will be trouble, but behold, I have overcome the world" (John 16:33)*. He was preparing his followers for his death, when they would go their own way, telling them that things aren't always as they first seem.

When we understand that hard may come first, we gain strength from knowing that something good beyond our wildest dreams may come down the pipeline. We see this in the disappointments and heartaches we face. Sometimes, they come in the form of health, and other times, they come as disappointment in sports, jobs, and relationships.

I once coached a player who was sure they were in love. After a charming courtship, they planned a beautiful wedding. Much to their surprise, and the surprise of everyone at the wedding, the plans changed moments before the ceremony began. The cancellation of the upcoming marriage was announced to a packed house just two minutes before the wedding was to take place. The minister told the congregation that the wedding was canceled, prayed for comfort, and dismissed the guests. Luckily, the would-be groom was long gone because the bride's competitive and athletic friends were unhappy about how this had played out.

The hurt, anger, and confusion ran deep. This was our teammate, someone we cared about. At the time, we didn't understand how something so bad could happen to someone so nice, but it was for the best. Marriage to the wrong person would have been far worse than a breakup on the wedding day. Of course, it would have been better if the decision had been made after the sixth date, but aren't we glad the decision was made and the bride didn't marry someone who didn't want to spend the rest of his life with her?

The couple broke up, and the bride and groom escaped to their separate ways. People of multiple generations were brokenhearted. However, as the years have passed, it has become evident that everything worked out for the best. There are new families and beautiful children on both sides. Everyone seems to be doing well. Forgiveness has also taken place. This is one of those instances where you learn that if a particular act can be forgiven, so can so many others. On the day of broken hearts, there was no way anyone could have predicted the power of forgiveness unless they had gone through something hard themselves. We need to know that we aren't always privy to understanding the more important purpose when a setback occurs. Forgiveness is such a powerful remedy for many things.

Paul addresses this in Romans 8:28. Scholars believe Paul was in prison when he wrote: *"And we know that in all things God works for the good of those who love him, who have been called according to his purpose" (NIV).* The Living Bible translates the verse this way: *"And we know that all that happens to us is working for our good if we love God and are fitting into his plans."*

I've experienced firsthand, many, many times, how good can come from challenging situations. I believe that Paul's words, written over two thousand years ago, were written for us so that we would trust that there is a plan with a big picture we are a living part of. I have repeatedly seen this in the lives of our players, my children, and God's children. My life is sometimes more difficult than I would like, and it has also been too good to be true. This is what makes life so unimaginably wonderful. When times are tough, we can believe that there's a purpose for it, and these tough times can be used for good.

Sports stories are usually about a struggle to overcome incredible odds. Some sports stories elicit our emotions because we identify with and admire the athletes as they fight their fears and insecurities. In fact, without trials, there is no story in sports or our lives outside of sports. Famous sports movies, such as *Rudy*, *Rocky*, *Secretariat*, and *Hoosiers*, tell captivating stories where the unfavored challenge the odds and come out on top. These tales bring us to the edge of our seats by breaking our hearts before capturing them later in the story. In these stories, there is almost always a pivotal moment when the subject reaches their breaking point but keeps going. Stories about a player or team that is the overwhelming favorite and goes on to win aren't as much fun to watch as the stories that involve overcoming challenges.

My love of sports brought me to my current job as a coach at Wofford College, one of the smallest Division I schools in the country, with men's tennis and scholarship football. Wofford is an unbelievable school with a rich athletic tradition of excellence. However, small comes with extensive tests. To paint a clearer picture, our school has just under two thousand students, while the average Division I school has 12,900 students. This is part of our story, but it isn't our focus. Although we're small, that is never an excuse; we compete to win. And we've gotten good at winning because we focus on our strengths.

Our players receive a fantastic experience in the categories that matter, such as community, attention from professors, and chances to compete at a high level. Due to how much we win as one of the smaller Division I schools, we often receive praise for doing more with less. I respect the coaches I work with because there is nothing easy about being small. If you're small and succeed, it is usually because you are wise, highly competitive, and tough as nails. I'm confident in stating that our tradition is to be all three.

Our players go on to professional baseball, basketball, football, golf, running, soccer, and tennis careers. Before coming to college, these players were typically labeled as not quite good enough to play at the highest level for one reason or another, yet they have proven their doubters wrong.

The professional athletes from Wofford remind our current athletes and people everywhere that you are only a finished product once you decide that growth is no longer worth it. College athletes can improve beyond their current level while still in school. They should never listen to negative inner voices and outside critics who tell them they cannot or won't jump to the next level. Their job is to grow their enthusiasm for their sport, never letting themselves become complacent. This mentality will serve them well in college and beyond.

Successful college athletes need grit and determination to take it to another level. This means doing things that not everyone thought you could do because you've never been there. Many people with disabilities have been given a list of things they'll never be able to accomplish. They play a demanding schedule daily, giving us the courage to play a great one, too. You can't fear losing and be willing to play a great schedule. Many people with special needs play to win every day.

We love seeing the stories of superstars who have overcome difficulties to make it to the big league. Most people who overcome challenges make it to the big league within their circumstances. The big league isn't necessarily the pros; it might be overcoming whatever you're dealing with. "Make the big league where you are" is one of my favorite sayings because it emphasizes that making the big league is about going for it wherever you are with everything you have, no matter the circumstance. Making the big time for some people might look like nothing for other people. This is why it is important not to judge others; we never know what they're overcoming.

At Wofford, our players have fantastic experiences where they grow intellectually and mature socially, and years later, they are successful and happy in the real world. In 23 years of coaching, I've only had three scholarship players transfer and play at another school. This is unheard of in the world of college sports. I don't take credit for our transfer rate because it is due to the total experience our school provides. When you join our school family, you learn to win on and off the field or court.

Our players graduate and move into incredible lives. This is precisely how the college athletic model is supposed to be. There is a lot to learn from how we do athletics. Academics come first, and our practice schedules are dictated by when classes are available for the student-athletes to take them. Amateur, from the Latin verb "amare," meaning to love or, in our case, for the love of the game—that is what college sports should be. This is sport in the purest form: two competing teams going at it for the love of the game and competition. Professional sports are a business and have a different purpose. The purpose of college sports is best modeled in an amateur fashion.

Less than two percent of college athletes play professionally, yet in many cases, the model is set up for them to become professional athletes both during and after college. Our model is set up for our players to become great students prepared for a lifetime of winning. We provide them with an excellent platform to soar into life. Why would anyone want to settle for anything less?

CHAPTER 8

An Amazing World

C oaching 18- to 22-year-olds is not an ordinary career. There is nothing normal about spending your entire work with this age group. It is super fun, but it isn't normal. They aren't kids anymore and are not quite adults yet, either. When their parents leave after dropping them off at college, their lives change quickly. It is often as if the young people automatically forget half of what they know to make room for new information.

This age group changes quickly, so coaches must adapt with them, or they'll get left behind quickly. Every year is different from the previous one because the actors change rapidly, and coaches never know what they will get. College coaching is a fast-paced, fun, and fantastic world, but you better believe in the merits of having a vocation over a profession.

Coaches who coach for their glory or ego make themselves and everyone around them miserable. They may have winning records, but that doesn't mean they impact lives. The only way to thrive in coaching is to do it for a purpose other than for yourself. People would be more fulfilled and happier if they looked for jobs based on what they felt called to do or what they believed they would enjoy instead of what might bring them other things. Gallup recently reported that 60 percent of people reported being emotionally detached at work, and 19 percent reported being miserable in their jobs.

I have a great job. It is a fantastic role centered around helping others get what they want. I feel joy crashing in like a roaring river when young people succeed. I can't imagine anything more meaningful and inspiring.

In coaching, personal relationships are everything. It is hard for me to get my hands around the fact that having friends and personal connections is especially tough for people with autism. When we received my son's diagnosis, my first thought was that it couldn't be true. He's turned out to be beautiful and lives an incredible life, but the journey has been a struggle.

Autism has taught me that life is full of things I can't control. This has allowed me to be happier and more resilient. I've learned to bend and not break by being more accepting of circumstances. I've learned to let go and live on life's terms. This is difficult for those of us who are highly competitive because everything matters to us. This is hard in athletics, too.

Most of the time, my best players are the most difficult to coach. They clash with other competitive players and are often stubborn regarding changes. Their strength is their weakness, and their weakness is their strength. This is because their story is what makes them good. Their story is what makes them persistent, focused, and strong-willed. Their story tells them that getting over losing will always be hard. However, while their story can be used for good, it often takes longer to get to the heart of what makes them tick.

Bear Bryant, the famous football coach at the University of Alabama, was known for his great life lessons and catchy sayings. Here's one of my favorites:

"I have always tried to teach my players to be fighters. When I say that, I don't mean put up your dukes and get in a fistfight over something. I'm talking about facing adversity in your life. There is not a person alive who isn't going to have some horrible days in their life. I tell my players that what I mean by fighting is when your house burns down, your wife runs away with the drummer, and you've lost your job, and all of the odds are against you. What are you going to do? Most people just lay down and quit. Well, I want my people to fight back."

This is a great message, and the intention is dead on. I've quoted this speech to players when we've faced difficult circumstances. Bryant's statement is classic. Fighting back when the hard times hit is the opposite of quitting. We know that quitters never win, and winners don't quit. However, a critical piece has been left out. This statement doesn't capture one of the essential survival parts: love. When everything seems like it is going against you, it is most important to have an attitude that demonstrates love for everyone. Autism has taught me a lot about love and forgiveness, lessons I needed to learn.

Take a minute and think of something difficult that has happened to you. It should be something personal that maybe you didn't see coming. Write this event down and describe it in three or four sentences. Next, consider the ways that you could have responded more lovingly. This is one type of resilience training that isn't talked about.

That love is the answer has been written in some of the world's most popular books. "Love is patient and kind, does not boast, isn't rude, and does not insist on its way" is a line that is often read at weddings. This statement doesn't say you should love when everything is going exceptionally well. Quite the contrary, it means loving when nothing is going right for you, and it describes explicitly what this love looks like.

I recently attended Kyle and Lida's wedding in Maiden, N.C. The venue, a 150-year-old secluded cotton mill, was a fantastic site for a wedding. The caterers carefully prepared the food, and the service went off without a hitch. In every way, the execution of the wedding was perfect.

As beautiful as the wedding was, what struck me the most was the message of unconditional love. It was a message I needed to hear. At five feet seven inches, Kyle was a giant among giants. We had a tall team in those years, but height isn't what makes a person a giant—it's loyalty, perseverance, toughness, and the ability to love unconditionally.

Kyle, a marine officer, loves well and doesn't quit when things get hard. Rather, he expects life to get hard, but that doesn't stop his love. My feelings had been hurt in the days leading up to the wedding, so the timing couldn't have been better. Quid pro quo shouldn't occupy space in relationships built on love. Though transactional relationships are often more manageable and cleaner than loving relationships, they are also less meaningful.

CHAPTER 9

The Gift of a Broken Heart

While the neurotypical children we knew were getting driver's licenses and developing socially, Cole was taking a different path. The disparity in social growth increased as many 15- and 16-year-olds became more independent, participating in more activities with their friends. I felt more alone than ever before. Nothing was happening in the ways that I had dreamed for my son.

I felt the pressure building as the number of questions grew about what life in the future would hold with an older child on the autism spectrum. This pressure darkened at a parent-teacher meeting when one of Cole's 9th-grade teachers told Merritt and me that he wasn't college material. The idea that Cole would never go to college had never crossed our minds because we have always believed in him. The teacher explained further that he didn't think Cole would ever drive.

Many in our community admired this teacher and school, but I felt betrayed by them. This conflict exasperated a loneliness that I didn't process well. The result manifested itself in anger and resentment that I should have caught, but the emotions regarding my son were raw and large. As a coach, I help players channel big emotions constructively. I could have used a great coach because I was drowning myself and didn't want anyone to know, leading to further isolation, disappointment, and anger.

Autism can be lonely because people don't think they know how to interact or connect with people with autism spectrum disorder (ASD), so they often do nothing to avoid failing at making a connection. We bring food when there's a death and flowers for a hospital stay, but we don't do much when there's an isolating condition. This results in loneliness.

Loneliness isn't reserved only for families with autism or disabilities. Currently, there's a crisis of loneliness. It doesn't discriminate, and social media isn't helping. Social media promotes fishbowl relationships where we see a picture, but the picture doesn't tell the story below the surface. Relationships are about what's below the surface of an event. Social media tricks us into believing an announcement tells the story. The result is that we compare what others show us on the outside to what we feel inside. This comparison is a setup because no one posts that they're lonely and having a hard time.

As my wife and I struggled with isolation, we adopted a dog to celebrate Cole's 16th birthday. We looked through the online dog adoption listings and agreed to look at a particular dog. Amid the chaos and uncertainty of our lives, we thought it would be a good idea to adopt the most enthusiastic beast we had ever seen. We were desperate to find a diversion from our challenges at home. This plan turned out to be a game-changer.

Merritt called an adoption agency, and the next thing I knew was that I needed to be home to meet a dog adoption case manager who had been sent to our house to identify if we could handle this unusually active dog. They warned us that his desire to play ball was over the top. As a college coach who has spent a lifetime playing ball, I thought this was perfect. The investigator examined our backyard and asked how active we were. After making a few notes, she left without divulging any information.

Our patience was tested as we waited five days before obtaining the green light from the agency. We were getting Luther, a full-grown, high-energy, bad-to-the-bone German Shepherd. We were ecstatic. However, we quickly learned that there was a lot that we didn't know about Luther.

Two days later, we were off to pick him up. I did not know much about German Shepherds then, but they're wired differently than your typical family pet. As soon as Luther jumped into the back of my truck, I was mesmerized. I had owned other dogs before, both large and small, but he was unlike anything I had experienced. Luther was one hundred percent muscle, and his teeth were huge. As we pulled away, I double-checked my rearview mirror to confirm that my kids weren't being eaten alive. However, Luther's size prevented me from seeing Cole and my other son, Ashe. I thought this might be part of Luther's purpose with us.

Luther had broad shoulders, a large, blocky head, and an enormous square jaw. German Shepherds are giant breeds, but Luther was massive. At a distance, he looked stunning, but up close, it was easy to see that he had many obstacles to overcome. His manager gave off a sour odor. He also had heartworms and a host of other issues. His numerous health problems came from him being chained to a fence and left alone behind a commercial warehouse as a guard dog. An animal rescue agency had saved him.

As we cared for Luther, regularly visited the vet, and paid more than four hundred dollars a month for his prescriptions, it became evident that our care for Luther was having an impact on us. Our minds were directed toward caring for something that needed our assistance. His sleek, athletic frame filled out to over 125 pounds as his health improved. The mange and skin odor were still evident to others, but we began to hardly notice it. His health problems were opportunities, and we began to have fun. We learned that caring for something or someone other than yourself is vitally important to living well. We should not focus on ourselves, even if we have problems. God used a mistreated dog to teach us this.

As we loved Luther, he took ownership of our home, especially our bed. He would place his enormous body diagonally so there was little room left. Merritt and I learned to race to our king-size bed every evening to see who could get there first, hoping we might salvage some leftover space. Luther seemed to enjoy absorbing every inch of the bed, and his gigantic frame was impossible to move. A crowded bed was a small price to pay for the jokes and laughter we enjoyed with this game. This was a happy time. Getting a big dog was exactly what we needed. To us, our sick and abused dog was the best-looking and most caring dog in the world.

I never worried about my family when I traveled overnight with the team because Luther was in charge at home. I told Merritt she could leave the house unlocked because there was no way anyone would break in with Luther inside. If anyone had entered our home, Luther would have thought, *It looks like someone wants to meet Jesus today*. There's no question Luther would have sacrificed his life for any of us.

Luther's mindset and loyalty were much like that of a great coach or boss who puts the needs of his people over his own, giving others the best parking spot and as much credit as possible. Empowering and lifting others is what coaching and leading are all about. Luther made a great coach.

The more we focused on taking care of Luther, the less we thought about autism and the problems overwhelming us. We discovered we could concentrate more on the joys that caring for others can provide. This breakthrough brought us happiness that I wish I had understood earlier. A seed had been planted. Life's purpose was beginning to shift.

Then, one day, Luther coughed up blood in our backyard. He was trembling in pain and could barely stand. He was very sick. Until that point, I had thought that Luther was eternally invincible. However, Luther was dying from an infection in his gut that was spreading quickly.

A week later, after two emergency surgeries, Merritt and I sobbed as we watched Luther pass away on the operating table. Unknown to us at the time, he had chewed up and eaten a tennis ball, which led to an infection in his digestive system that had spread.

The timing of Luther's death couldn't have been worse. Caring for him had brought our family together in a difficult time. He was the glue that held us together and brought light to a dark time in our lives. When Luther died, Cole was visiting my parents in North Carolina, and Ashe was at a tennis tournament in Mobile, Alabama. It would have been better for our children to go through Luther's death with us. Their grieving process would have been more straightforward and less misunderstood if they'd had a chance to say goodbye.

Merritt and I weren't equipped to talk about Luther's death over the phone, so we waited three days to break the news. This was a strange time, and we felt vulnerable. Ashe was beginning to spend more time at a tennis academy away from home, and we sensed a need to bring our family together.

Due to the timing, Luther's death took my breath away. Events have meaning that correlates to where we are in our personal lives. For example, when two young people get cut from the same team in the same year, they will often respond in entirely different ways. One might hang it up and move on, while the other will become more driven and motivated. Two years later, one might be the league's MVP, while the other rarely considers the sport anymore. The same event produces entirely different responses because of the uniquely personal experiences that led up to it.

We knew that Luther's death would be a difficult adjustment, so we acted quickly. The next day, we got up before sunrise and found puppies available nearby. We soon signed our recruit. When our children came home, we were excited to introduce them to Lexi, our new German Shepherd puppy.

Lexi was different from Luther. She was eight weeks old, and we had gotten to play and interact with her beautiful parents. Lexi came with a pedigree. She had sweet puppy breath and tiny teeth. Her health wasn't in question. Lexi was an ace. We were confident she would help us overcome our sadness and mend our broken hearts.

We were about to be introduced to one of life's classic lessons: things aren't always as they seem, especially when it involves families. Ashe was devastated that we had brought Lexi home and wanted nothing to do with her. His loyalty was to Luther, and he was insulted that we had replaced Luther so quickly because Luther was family. Ashe's disappointment devastated us, but we knew he was right for feeling the way he did. It felt like when a child's parent dies, and the other parent remarries quickly. The child's allegiance is to the deceased mother or father.

Although our intentions were pure, bringing Lexi into our home without including our boys in the decision was a mistake. Our family needed time to grieve before we could accept Lexi. Grief showed itself through anger, isolation, and confusion.

Learning to grieve has been an essential part of our family's story, and the grief isn't just about Luther. We grieve because life isn't how we thought it would be. It's important to learn that we do not control how life should or will be. We're not in charge of directing life. We've also learned that grief isn't cured with replacement or diversion. We had to mourn not only Luther's death but also what we had assumed life would be like.

Luther's life reminds me of C.S. Lewis's *The Lion, the Witch and the Wardrobe*.[20] Luther came into our family and helped us find happiness and joy. C.S. Lewis wrote about Aslan, the mighty lion of Narnia who gave his life to save the young boy Edmund. Although I believe he would have, Luther didn't intentionally die for us as Aslan did, but we learned a lot through his death. When Aslan returns the troubled brother to Peter and his siblings, he says, "Here is your brother, and there is no need to talk with him about what is past." Aslan takes this moment to teach the children about forgiveness. The crux of the whole story is about forgiveness and love. When there is real hurt, you can learn about forgiveness and love in a profound, lasting way.

Luther had advantages due to his size and commanding presence, but his life had gotten off to a rough start. You couldn't tell from the outside looking in, but Luther's health problems made him vulnerable. I can't help but wonder if they made him kinder to those who took care of him.

There's much to be learned from those with perceived disadvantages. Luther didn't have a pedigree. He wasn't fancy. He was a big dog, no better or worse than any other. He lived below the radar in many ways, an advantage because of how it lets you see the world. Colors look more vivid, mountains taller, and smiles more endearing because you're not consumed with yourself. When you're below the radar, you tend to think less about yourself and more about others.

CHAPTER 10

Make Room for the Enemy

P eople are sometimes left out of events or gatherings for no apparent reason that makes sense. Another name for this is marginalization. Race, poverty, disability, socioeconomic standing, and religion are all reasons people are marginalized. Sometimes, marginalization is blatant, and other times, it is subtle. Everyone loses when marginalization happens.

Neurodiversity, which embraces autism as a different way of thinking or seeing the world, provides an answer to the problem of marginalization. In her article "What Is Neurodiversity?" posted on the Harvard Health Publishing website, Nicole Baumer, M.D., writes, "Neurodiversity describes the idea that people experience and interact with the world around them in many different ways; there is no one 'right' way of thinking, learning, and behaving, and differences are not seen as defects."[21] When explained this way, it is easy to believe that including the neurodiverse population would be beneficial because it exposes us to new ideas.

Why do we leave some people out when including them is easier and kinder? Is it because we suspect our event will be more manageable without them? Do we think they don't want to go? I'll never know the answers to these questions, but I do know that considering these questions has challenged me to seek ways to include others. Including only those who can do something for us makes the relationship transactional. Relationships are supposed to be loving and kind, not transactional.

What if the one left out is your child? I remember when someone once told me that a person with autism didn't seem to want friends. I was shocked because this person, who thinks they're smart, actually believed this. This comment reminded me how important it is never to assume that I know what someone else wants. Making friends is more challenging for some people than others, but everyone deserves and desires friends.

Sometimes, making friends can be the hardest thing for someone to do. I may not be able to swim across the Atlantic Ocean because I don't have those skills, but that doesn't mean I don't want to. A person with autism who doesn't have many friends might wish to have one very badly. There are so many opportunities for kindness, to demonstrate to someone who may not have many friends that they are your best friend.

When it came to my son, I had to love those who left him out, or it would've killed me. I had to look for ways to include people and never be bitter when he didn't receive the treatment he deserved. It was hard, but that's what getting back up means.

Do you mean to tell me I have to love people who leave out my child? Exactly! That's precisely whom I need to love, and I better have an urgency about it. If not, I'll get back up fighting, and the anger inside will kill me.

This is the stuff that ruins lives and is one of the primary reasons so many marriages with special needs children come to an end. But they don't have to end this way. Love can overcome hate, but it takes a conscious effort. The secret no one talks about is that love must remain when you are knocked down and get back up.

The internal stress beats you down, and you get angry because you're worn out. The stress comes from the most personal level and builds up. This is why a consistent approach to love and forgiveness is necessary. While Love will deescalate tension to a manageable level, hatred will escalate it. Hatred is a warning sign that we should look at what is happening inside ourselves.

Rivalries are essential in college sports. However, you can't have ill will for your rival and be happy. You can root for your team when they play, but you shouldn't root against the opponent, and it should never be personal. You must want the best for your rival, or your feelings will eat your heart away.

I see this in sports all the time; taking the rival personally never helps the player. We should pull for our team but not hate the other team even if they discriminate against us. Maybe your rival is someone you work with or possibly a family member. It is likely someone who either has something you'd like to have or someone you feel doesn't give you enough credit.

We're seeing this us-versus-them mentality a lot in our country right now. People either take the side of CNN or Fox. Such an attitude can't be correct because we know each side has both good and not-so-good features. Our job is to see the good in others, which is impossible when we believe one side has all the answers. Love doesn't exist in this form.

Whoever or whatever your rival is, pull for them. I started doing this a few years ago, and the results have been excellent. I've gone from angry to understanding. Don't get me wrong, I want to win more than ever, but I want the other team to win, too. This new way of thinking hasn't diminished my competitive spirit. Quite the opposite; it has helped me focus on what I need to focus on, making life much more fun and productive. In all likelihood, my rivals are dealing with their own challenges. This perspective gives me a better chance of having one of the greatest characteristics: empathy for others.

I'm glad to see the other team and their coaches when we're on the road. I'm a better coach and person when I wish them the best. Amazingly, I learned this from the autism community. In the special needs arena, we want everyone to win in the biggest way possible. Sports isn't any different, and it certainly isn't more critical.

Wanting the best for rivals has had a positive impact on my team. Here's an example. On Christmas, Ashe and I spent the day at the airport as flights continued to be delayed. We were waiting for a player from one of our rival teams, ETSU, currently top in our league. One of their best players is from Argentina, and he couldn't go home for Christmas, so he spent nine days at our house. He eats tuna from a can. He's a tough kid. He's glad to be in America. Hard worker. Doesn't own a car. I like him. We hosted the enemy and enjoyed his company. Not only that, but he and Ashe practiced their faces off over Christmas break. We all want to win, but we helped each other. This is how it's supposed to work. Make room for the other guy in the inn, especially on Christmas. Work hard, be humble, forgive quickly, and laugh often.

Good coaches are empathetic. It is hard to be a good person without empathy. Some people believe it takes authentic, active listening, but that's only the beginning. You also have to see the person's story from their viewpoint. Good friends can do this, and it is hard to be one without demonstrating empathy.

I've become better at navigating difficulty through my experiences in the special needs arena. Has the same thing happened to you because of your experiences in other spaces? Think for a minute about what you have overcome. Isn't this an essential part of what makes you who you are? If so, shouldn't these experiences be celebrated? They should, but only if we can find a way to use them for good. There is a way; we have to look for it.

Such moments can be learning opportunities, so don't miss them. One of mine came in the form of a child's autism diagnosis. Yours could be something completely different, but you have them, too. You've had them before and will undoubtedly have them again. It might be job loss, cancer, divorce, a broken relationship, or anything that causes grief or heartbreak.

My goal is to help you be prepared for when the next worst thing hits. If we get this right, the next worst thing will take us to a higher level of thinking, communication, and action so we can pivot into a life of power and live for a higher, more meaningful reason. When the next worst thing strikes, we'll be ready. We'll feel the joy of improved relationships and living in a new way. When you face challenging times, you will no longer strive to escape them but embrace them as defining moments that create new life. We'll see the world through a new set of eyes. We won't live in fear but in service to a greater purpose. How does this sound? It takes implementation and action to make it happen, but a life like this isn't too good to be true. It doesn't matter if you coach, sell tires, or make pharmaceuticals. Pull for other people, and you will venture down a road of impactful living.

A sign in my office reads, "Intense competition makes us better." Do we live this way? Warriors aren't afraid of losing. We know we can grow stronger from facing tough challenges and opponents, but only if we are willing to change. Some say that adversity makes us stronger. This isn't always true. Adversity can make us stronger, but it can also hurt us by killing our confidence and making us bitter. Intense competition can mold us, and adversity can make us stronger. These are growth tools, but they don't work if they stay in the toolbox. You have to take them out and use them.

Someone recently told me that they wanted their faith to grow. The question to ask yourself is, why would you like your faith to grow? Or why do you want something? Maybe you're unhappy, and you want to be happy. Or you're not in great shape and want to improve your fitness.

Having a special needs child can help you grow, but it can also cause pain, anger, or denial. I was at such a loss that I was forced to lean into God and grow. I opted to accept things that I couldn't control. I could have focused on the negatives, which common sense tells us isn't productive. I was fortunate, and I want others going through tough times to have even better fortune after their difficulties. This is a big part of *Hard Comes First.*

Whatever the challenge is, we can learn to embrace it as a mechanism for growth. Great golfers enjoy challenging courses more than easy ones. For example, the Ocean Course on Kiawah Island is often rated as one of the best golf courses in South Carolina and one of the most difficult. A commentator for *Golf Digest* writes:

"The 17th hole is the toughest par 3 in the world. If the wind blows, watch out. The course is challenging for all levels of player. When the wind is blowing, par is an excellent score. If your idea of a good time is a fistfight, this is the place for you."[22]

In its list of difficult courses, ESPN states, "The Ocean is a rare breed that can bring tears and fears to the pros."[23] Challenging courses are more thrilling for skilled competitors, and they can also demand a higher fee. In other words, we are willing to pay for the challenge because we love the competition.

Skilled kayakers prefer navigating aggressive rapids over clear streams. Athletic teams feel more accomplished when they beat the best than when they defeat the worst. Tennis takes many years of year-round playing to become an advanced player. This is precisely why it is one of the most popular sports in the world.

This is how competitive people are wired, so it is no secret that we should pursue complex tasks to bring out our best. We enjoy challenges. Once we've paid our dues, it is hard for us to quit. However, we are rarely fully invested when things are easy to accomplish. Meaningful satisfaction is gained after we have pushed through difficulty.

Meaningful satisfaction is worth examining to understand our purpose and how we interact with people at work and in our personal lives. A recent

Gallup poll shows that only 48 percent of people in the U.S. are happy with their current job.[24] However, this statistic does not tell the critical part of the story. What's important is what's found in another Gallup poll, which shows that 68 percent of employees are not engaged in their work.[25] We come to work, check-in, do a job, and leave without feeling inspired. This is where we find the hidden disconnect. Most folks don't mind hard work as long as they're inspired, but we don't prioritize inspiration as one of the primary goals of the workplace.

In a *Harvard Business Review* article titled "Why Inspiration Matters," Scott Kauffman writes:

"Inspiration increases well-being. In another study, those exposed to Michael Jordan's greatness experienced higher levels of positive affect, and their score on the Inspiration Scale completely explained this increase in positive affect. However, this inspiration was not transitory, predicting positive well-being (e.g., positive affect, life satisfaction) three months later! Inspiration was more strongly related to the future than to present satisfaction. Self-reported levels of purpose and gratitude in life explained the extent to which inspiration lasted."[26]

Thrash and Elliot developed the Inspiration Scale, which measures the frequency with which a person experiences inspiration in their daily lives. They found that inspired people were more open to new experiences and reported more absorption in their tasks. "Openness to experience" often came before inspiration, suggesting that those more open to inspiration are likelier to experience it.[27]

Here's the big takeaway from Kauffman's ideas. Inspiration lasts when we are inspired to have purpose and gratitude. This is remarkable. Great leaders help us be thankful for our experiences. Having a purpose above and beyond your desires and being grateful for the opportunity to serve others bring people joy and meaning to their lives.

Most people who play Division I tennis have never been on a team before coming to college. They traveled with their families and friends and competed without teammates. It is a super competitive but isolating environment. Many find it to be lonely. In a perfect world, young people should play both team and individual sports. The two teach entirely different skill sets.

Team sports teach people how to work together and share the spotlight. Players learn to pull for the person who has the spot they'd like to have. They learn to sacrifice for a common goal. Individual sports teach people to rely on themselves. They can't blame others for their losses. Goal setting is very inward-focused. This is not how we are supposed to live.

College tennis is a team sport. Although it takes college players time to adjust, most people overwhelmingly prefer the team format over the individual format. This makes sense. We like to play for something bigger than ourselves. However, this doesn't come automatically to people who have been brought up playing only individual sports. Unfortunately, some players never get it until after graduation, when it seems too late, but it isn't too late at all. Life is richer and more fun when we serve others. The sooner we understand this, the happier we will be. Join the team and keep diving into giving more. Seek ways to help others beyond your level of comfort.

Adults can live as if they have a team, too. Teamwork doesn't have to end when college is over. If being on a team sounds rewarding, make your own team right where you are. Be diligent in reaching out and being there. Pull for people and look for ways to inspire, encourage, and love them even if you don't think they need you. Some families operate like teams. Someone acts as "team captain" while the other "players" take on supporting roles. Making a team without a formal structure and name is possible with a little effort and intentionality.

"To whom much is given, much is required" - Luke 12:48. This passage has been used to motivate people to be better citizens of various communities,

businesses, teams, and countries. Human nature leads us to feel that we should serve ourselves first. Once we have enough power, money, prestige, notoriety, etc., then we can give more to others. This is completely backward. Instead, we should give more to others than ourselves from the beginning.

Tennis players are typically highly competitive, but sharing doesn't always come naturally for them. For example, a few years ago, I received a phone call from a player's parent whose son, a freshman, wasn't getting the playing time he thought he deserved. The parent warned me that the player would quit if he didn't get more playing time and wasn't put in the starting lineup more often.

The well-intentioned parent thought he was being helpful. I was shocked but said nothing. The real problem with this scenario is twofold: the parent didn't think their child's ego could handle not playing, and they didn't believe their child had enough fight to earn playing time. The parents had worked hard to make their child's life as easy as possible, so neither child nor parent believed in the value of a team. The good news is that the player grew and eventually earned playing time on their merit, but it was a struggle.

We are encouraged to act as individuals but enjoy corporate success more. Deep inside, we long to be helpful, kind, and appreciated by our teammates, coworkers, and friends. We need to be part of something larger than ourselves. There's no escaping it because that is how we are designed.

Two essential characteristics for college athletes are drive and determination. A good coach will nurture players' desires so their drive to achieve optimal performance increases. This is also the goal of a proficient manager or leader. Being a good coach or manager helps us to enjoy what we're doing so we keep growing and striving for better results for the people we work with.

A fun and rewarding environment is more likely to keep motivation high. However, this is difficult to accomplish in isolation. Maintaining relationships and investments in other people is one of the most proven tactics to keep one's fire burning. Everyone needs a team to have the drive to stay alive and be sustained for the long haul.

The best way to build a team is to devote energy, purpose, and interest to others. Some people wait for the team to find them. This doesn't work. Everyone is responsible for building their team, even if it isn't a formal one. Building a team is about caring for others. Who is on the team that you've made? Start building your team today. It is never too late to do so.

College athletes sometimes need more motivation during their college careers. This is especially true during their senior year if there's a threat of reduced playing time. Good teammates finish the race, but this is rarely emphasized by society or parents. One must be unselfish to endure the ups and downs of disappointments. It is also the job of a good coach and team culture to keep the players locked into finishing, even with the many distractions that seem essential. The race lasts four years, and each year has a uniquely different role. Emphasis needs to be placed on starting the race and finishing strong. The same is true in other endeavors.

How important is motivation? Jim Taylor, Ph.D., writes in *Psychology Today*, "Motivation will impact performance. It is also the only factor over which you have control. Motivation will directly impact the level of success that you ultimately achieve."[28] This is true in sports, work, and personal lives. When a young coach recently asked me how I stayed so positive, I replied that I'm optimistic because I work on it. Negativity is easy, and it hurts motivation. If you want to be motivated, you need to work very hard at it.

Early in my coaching career, a highly regarded athletic administrator told me he believed high-character college athletes desire to be part of a demanding program. I've thought about that statement throughout my career and believe it to be true. Everyone desires engagement beyond money and material possessions. We all long to be part of something special or selective. For instance, after a rigorous practice, teams gain a sense of pride in returning to the dorm and telling their friends, "Wow, you wouldn't believe what we did today." This is especially true when it is a team where the players have set expected and acceptable standards.

I've never had a player look back at their college athletic experience and think, *I wish I hadn't worked so hard.* We gain satisfaction from completing difficult and complex tasks. The U.S. Marine Corps has built a spirit of pride in their corps on this concept. Undoubtedly, we gain a sense of satisfaction in growing through challenging situations. You don't have to be a Marine to gain confidence. Sometimes, the most challenging times are when we show up, keep moving forward, or never quit on someone we care about.

CHAPTER 11

Skin in the Game

G reat parenting, just like exceptional leadership, takes engagement. Although parenting can be fun, most people agree it isn't easy. However, people can agree that it is one of the most rewarding parts of their life. Young people look forward to parenting, and older people reminisce about the days when their children were young. I've heard it said of parenting that "the days are long, but the years go by fast." This is true with anything we pour ourselves into, be it parenting, sports, starting a business, or attending graduate school. College students often state that their time in college flies by after their freshman year.

Parenting is uniquely different for the family of a child with autism. According to the documentary *Autism Every Day*, shows divorce rates for parents of children with autism are as high as 80 percent, compared to an average divorce rate of around 25 percent for first marriages.[29] Many critics have debated the accuracy of the number, but everyone can agree that families with special needs are constantly under what feels like insurmountable stress. More recent research indicates that families with autism have a divorce rate that is closer to ten percent higher than the norm.[30] Experts all agree that the stress levels for families with autism are tremendous.

For parents of special needs children, the years are often marked with an atypical amount of stress and uncertainty. The degree of required unselfishness is higher than the norm. The low moments are more frequent, deeper, and wider than in typical marriages. However, this is where the gift lies. The goal of living well is to reach a level of unselfishness where accolades no longer matter. The same is true with being a great boss or coach. Once we learn to give our lives away, we gain more than we could have ever believed.

Relationships become more valuable with a higher level of investment when you have skin in the game. This saying comes from horse racing, where the owners have a lot to win or lose. Warren Buffet made the phrase famous when he spoke about using his money to begin his original fund.

The same is true in sports. The more you invest in your sport, the more rewarding it becomes. Growing a business from scratch is more rewarding than being a number at a large company. Attending graduate school on your dime is more fulfilling than graduating from the seventh grade. There's evidence that everything is more rewarding when you've invested more, but that doesn't mean it comes without pain.

When you parent a child with autism, you have "skin in the game." This can make you a better person, or it can break you. The stress can rip you apart. Everyone agrees that parenting can be challenging even with neurotypical children, but when there's a special needs child, the stress can easily triple.

Each stage of parenting is different. Some early years require a lot of physical support, such as feeding and changing diapers. The early school years present some stress but are generally happy times. The early teenage years present challenges with new amounts of uncertainty. The late teens and early 20s are typically years of excitement and growth. For a family with an autistic child, these groupings don't exist. You learn to celebrate the success of others while your child is on the outside looking in. The parent is often the child's only connection to the world. In these cases, the parent has a lot of "skin in the game."

A child with special needs may not be able to do some of the things other children can do, but that is only part of it. Often, the things that can't be seen are the most difficult. These are the things that wear people down emotionally. You can't help but wonder why the child won't act or behave a certain way. At some point, you must accept that the rules of your game aren't the ones you've chosen, but they're still the ones in front of you.

Every sport has rules that make it the game that it is. Some sports are unique because you can only score when batting or serving. Other sports, like basketball, football, and soccer, have a clock. In sports with a clock, you can sometimes build up enough of a lead so the opposing team doesn't have time to make a comeback.

Tennis is one of the sports that does not have a clock. The first player to win six games wins the set, and the first player to win two sets wins the match. The winner must score last, so you can always come from behind and win. For example, we had a player who lost the first set 6-0 and went down 5-0 in the second set. At that point, he pumped his fist and yelled, "Come on, baby! I've got him right where I want him!" At that moment, the fans, referees, coaches, and teammates could feel the momentum shift. His walk transformed into a powerful strut, his shoulders broadened, and he beamed confidently. His shots gained a more penetrating bite, and his footwork was more tenacious than ever. It was game on all the way. He had found his groove, and his play rose to a higher level.

The opposing player had failed to clamp down when he had the chance. That opportunity had vanished forever. I sensed that the opposing player was saying to himself, "There's a new sheriff in town, and I'm uncomfortable. This is going to be complicated." Our player stepped on the gas and came back to win that set 7-5 and then ran away with a routine third set to close the match. The opponent was demoralized. When the match shifted from easy to hard, his game evaporated.

Our player got better that day, and the opposing player could have, too. The right mindset can allow us to reinvent ourselves in difficult times. In fact, without difficulties, it is almost impossible to grow into who we can become.

Being unable to devise a viable solution can be frustrating. Maybe we're coming out of difficulty and don't have an answer for the next step. Or perhaps we were in a good place, but we let it slip away without seizing the momentum. Such times can make us feel like failures. This feeling is normal because we're now in a new and uncomfortable situation. Winning athletes learn to handle these awkward situations better than most because they can stay neutral.

Life is often like a tennis match, where a single moment can change the momentum of our day, week, year, and even life. This is precisely why we must instill the discipline of seeking momentum opportunities.

This is so true in a tennis match. You must learn to focus on the point that is right in front of you. This is a learned skill for most of us. Fear, worry, and anxiety about what may or may not happen are not part of a winning equation. We can get better at navigating the uncomfortable, but it takes experience and practice. We can't be afraid of discomfort if we want to live a life of growth.

College sports can be emotionally and physically brutal. For example, one of our hardest-working and most dedicated players faced disappointment. Playing college tennis had been his dream. He trained tirelessly, and he and his family made great sacrifices to allow him to become a Division I college athlete.

Once he got to college, he improved his fitness by paying attention to every detail of his diet, training, and recovery. In the summers, he trained tenaciously to gain an edge and did everything expected of an elite player. He left no stone unturned in giving himself a chance to reach his potential.

However, each of his first two college seasons was cut short due to injury, and he suffered another season-ending injury in his third year.

He's not the same person he was when he joined us, demonstrating perseverance through one blow after another. It is too early to tell whether these injuries will positively or negatively impact his life, but knowing him, I believe the net impact will be positive. At some point in the future, he will likely be in a leadership position where he can help someone fight through discouragement. I hope that he'll lean into his experiences and be impactful.

Net Impact is an important concept to understand when we deal with difficulty. In business or accounting, the net impact is the final result after all the debits and credits are considered. We are not privileged to know the net impact of everything we do, so we are wise to stay neutral like a great athlete under pressure.

A story I heard about a poor tenant farmer in China has helped me to keep a proper perspective. The poor farmer worked someone else's land with someone else's tools and lived in someone else's house. When the crops went to market, he had to pay a steep tithe to the owner. He owned nothing except a beloved horse who helped the family plow the fields to earn a meager living.

One day, the horse ran away, and the farmer's neighbors exclaimed, "Your horse ran away! What terrible luck!" The farmer replied, "Maybe so, maybe not." A few days later, the horse returned home, leading a herd of wild horses back to the farm. The neighbors shouted, "Your horse has returned and brought many horses home! You are now the richest horse owner in town! What great luck you have!" The farmer calmly replied, "Maybe so, maybe not."

The following week, the farmer's son was trying to break one of the horses, and it threw him to the ground, fracturing his leg in multiple places. The damage was so bad that the boy could no longer walk. The people in the village cried, "Your son broke his leg! What terrible luck!" The farmer replied, "Maybe so, maybe not."

A few weeks later, soldiers from the emperor's army marched through town, recruiting all boys for war. They did not take the farmer's son because he had a lame leg. All the other young men were led to the front line of battle, where they would face a perilous death. The neighbors shouted, "Your boy is spared! What tremendous luck!" To which the farmer replied, "Maybe so, maybe not."

The farmer knew that he did not have all the answers to how life would play out. This gave him great freedom. We've discussed staying in the process while you are in the storm. Be where your feet are, not in the past, not in the future, but right in the moment where you are. This takes emotional discipline. Good coaches, bosses, friends, and spouses help us to see the merits of living where our feet are. They lead by example and teach us in their journey.

For a transformational experience, we must be all in. Only then can we learn to live, rebound, and recover from disappointment. This is one of the fundamental reasons that college athletics is an excellent investment in our society.

Parents with children with autism must become strong at staying focused on doing the next right thing. It is easy to go down the path of forecasting what might happen or what could have been. This behavior is destructive because we miss out on the good we might otherwise see. The particular challenge doesn't matter. It could be cancer, job loss, or any other obstacle.

When recruiting new prospects, I often ask them to describe their most significant challenge. By understanding what causes their sleepless nights, I can better coach them. Getting to know people below the surface is one of the most critical challenges coaches face. Players have different pressures for various reasons and are not immune to responding to those pressures in the crunch.

Life is not about our favorite car or vacation spot. Instead, it is about the experiences that shape us. These issues almost always involve people, relationships, and adversity. This process continues throughout their college playing career. Young people deal with a lot of stress, and I cannot coach them well if I do not understand the anxieties and fears they are wrestling with. This is especially true in tennis because the sport pits one player against another, bringing many feelings to the surface. It's crucial to learn about the stress behind the action.

Learning about people at a deeper level isn't limited to college athletics. It is about having relationships that matter. It is about heart and caring for one another. Like anything important, it takes time, energy, and mental resources. Coaching gives you this opportunity, but it exists everywhere if we want it.

In competition, we learn about our opponent's negative emotions by evaluating their body language after they've made a mistake or we make a big play. Sloping shoulders, withdrawn expressions, and sagging eyes are a few of the cues we read. We can also hear it in our teammates' tones when they feel discouraged. We must be proactive in rising to the occasion and picking up teammates. Life is too short to do anything less.

Empathy is an essential part of being a teammate or coach and necessary for any relationship with substance. To be able to put yourself in someone else's shoes is one of life's greatest privileges. Someone who lacks this ability or desire is missing out on one of life's best experiences: having caring relationships with others. This is hard to accomplish without empathy.

College athletics provides a fantastic platform for teaching what's right, but that is not what is always emphasized. Everyone wants to be aligned with a winner, but the opportunity lies with how we define winning. Even great college athletes are often not equipped to help each other with the challenge of disappointment, but it is a profound skill that can be taught and learned. This is why college athletics has such an incredible value when done right.

There's a lot of pressure for college athletics to be done wrong. Ethical behavior is everyone's responsibility, but it isn't always rewarded materially. However, it is rewarded with the things that matter in life, like meaningful and trustworthy relationships. The high stakes in college sports mean the opportunities for equipping young people to be good citizens are vast. Making ethical decisions based on what is right and kind is what matters the most when the stakes are high.

Although injuries are often outside our control, one of the things we can control in college athletics is the strength of our non-conference schedule. In essence, you can control a portion of your win-loss record with the quality of your opponents. We play a demanding schedule because challenging competition is one of the things you need to take your game to another level.

You also get to choose your strength of schedule in the real world. Life can wear you down and make you want to play an easier schedule by shutting people out and creating walls. Or you can live and love to the fullest no matter what comes your way. We were created to live with a vibrant schedule. The key is maintaining a heart full of hope for yourself and others. This will determine essential things about you, such as who your friends are and how you allocate your free time. Being a person of risk does not mean you make dangerous choices. Quite the opposite, it means you spend your time doing things that have meaning and add value to others.

Life can be challenging, but that shouldn't scare us. Mantras such as "When the going gets tough, the tough get going" rally us to fight when we face a setback. This battle cry tells us to do something quickly when the opponent scores or when we make a mistake. Be present and know that the comeback must always be more remarkable than the setback. Comebacks outside the arena of sports can take months or years, but no matter how long it takes, momentum, perseverance, and courage are needed to turn things around. Embrace the comeback for yourself and others.

CHAPTER 12

Happiness

We naturally cling to our past because that is all we know. One moment, however, taught me that the future is a lot more critical than the past. Upon learning of our son Cole's diagnosis, my wife and I embarked on a journey to help him. All bets were off; we would help him no matter what it took. My background in athletics supports this attitude. When there's a problem, work hard until you get it right. When you fail, get back up and keep working hard. Keep your eye on the ball and keep going. Sports are fantastic. You know the game's rules, and playing is your job. Real life doesn't play by fair rules, which has repeatedly broken my heart.

I had choices to consider. Was my life supposed to be focused on my perceived needs? This was my time to grow up and become a leader. Although I was about 40 when Cole was diagnosed, I was still a kid in many ways.

Cole's autism has taught me a lot. One of the most important things I've learned is how selfish I am. Our society teaches us to be self-absorbed in many ways. Advertising makes us believe that we deserve or need something, that our kids are the center of the universe, or that we should have whatever we want if we work hard enough. None of these ideas are true. My selfishness was making me miserable. Since then, my purpose has become laser-focused: to take care of all of God's kids, not just my own.

We do a tremendous disservice to college students when we tell them they can become anything they want. It is true that with hard work, people can achieve great things and pursue almost any career. However, this should not mean that getting what we wish will fulfill us, make us happy, or be our reason for living. There's no way that someone between the ages of 18 and 22 has the knowledge or wisdom to discern what or who they hope to be when they get older. The better answer is that we can become who we should be with hard work, focus, and thoughtful consideration. I do not believe we should become self-absorbed and selfish people. This is a one-way ticket to misery.

Before Cole's autism diagnosis, my biggest concern was how I would get my needs filled. Everything was planned out, and life was moving nicely in the direction I thought would make me the most comfortable. Although I was checking off boxes, I did not feel that I was growing or living in joy. I have realized that self-seeking does not correlate with meaningfulness or happiness.

I was never a bad person. I have always cared about others and had many friends. That is not the point. The point I want you to understand is that motive matters most.

If you are currently unhappy at work or in your personal life, try helping three people who cannot do anything for you. Here are some steps to get you started. Try them for a month and then adjust them as you see fit.

1. Think about three people you know who cannot do anything for you. Here are some examples:
    a. An unappealing, unpopular neighbor.
    b. Someone at work with whom others have disdain because they're difficult to get along with.
    c. The lonely-looking person who works at the station where you buy gas.

2. Write down their names on a list and place them somewhere you'll see them daily.

3. Commit to serving these people for five weeks. This means that you will help them without expecting anything in return. Every day, you should do something nice for one of them. Rotate through your list to hit each one at least once every three days. Here are some examples:

    a. Invest in them by calling them once a week without an agenda.
    b. Go out of your way to do nice things for them. You can give them something or do something nice for them. Make sure that you sacrifice in some way.
    c. Pay them compliments.
    d. If you have a particular gift, such as being good with finances, fitness, art, etc., use it to help them.

These steps will get your focus off you and your troubles and onto those who can't do anything for you. There cannot be any ulterior motive other than kindness for the sake of service. When I first mentioned three people, you likely thought that was a few, but after you read the requirements, you might have thought you would need more time for three. I promise three will not be enough once you make it a habit.

We are going to learn more about this later. For now, please focus on helping the people on your list. If you want a more meaningful life, give this exercise a good shot.

This thought goes with what a wise carpenter told his friends years ago about praying for their enemies. When we do nice things for others who cannot do anything for us, there's no guarantee that our gesture will help them, but it will almost always help us.

From my years of experience working on a college campus, I estimate that 70 percent of all college freshmen tell someone, like a best friend or parent, that they want to transfer. It might happen after they fail their first series of tests, get left out of a group, or don't get the playing time they'd immediately like. However, most don't act on it. Thus, they learn resiliency, but only if they learn humility first. The humility gained from the experience of failure teaches resiliency.

Kids with autism get left out often because people do not know what to do with them. When Cole was in the third grade, someone told me he did not act like he wanted to have friends because he played alone. Another time, he was the only child in a class not invited to a birthday party. These are not isolated experiences; they happen often with kids with autism. I share these experiences because they are common for people with ASD. As awareness increases, the hope is that incidents like these will become rarer.

When your child gets left out, you can become bitter or better. I admit that my journey to getting better has been a trial. I was angry for years, and it hurt me. Bitterness serves no constructive purpose and only does damage. However, overcoming bitterness has improved me in every life category, including marriage, friends, and coaching. I've become much better at taking people as they are. There's just no other way to live.

Early in my coaching career, I remember thinking, "If my players do not play better, I will be stuck at this school forever." What a terrible thing to consider. I cannot imagine playing on a team with a coach who thought like this. I was not a very good coach when I started because I was selfish. It is said that many people in America are unhappy with their jobs. They don't enjoy their work, and job satisfaction is low. I understand this because, although I have had great careers, there have been times when I have been unhappy. However, life has a purpose that supersedes the pursuit of happiness.

Happiness has a lot to do with being thankful. Have you ever met someone who is genuinely thankful all the time? What is it about such people? Research indicates that gratitude and thankfulness are skills. By definition, skills can be learned, unlike talents or gifts, which are typically considered traits we are born with.

As with any skill, we learn thankfulness by committing ourselves to rigorous practice. People who are thankful enjoy better health, relationships, and productivity, so putting in the daily work of thankfulness is worth it.

Our team had practice on the Friday before Thanksgiving break when 95 percent of the students had left campus. The players came together at the end of training, put their hands in a circle, and chanted, "One, two, three, thankful. One, two, three, thankful." As we dispersed, I couldn't help but smile when I realized the young man leading the chant had his arm in a brace. He's faced the disappointment of injury, yet he continues to work hard and be thankful. The team is full of guys who've faced disappointment and gotten stronger because they never quit. After practice, they broke bread together, played poker, and shared many laughs.

Our team is exceptional. We smell like smoke because we've been through more than our share of fires, but we're becoming rock solid. We're thankful. And there's a secret we're not telling our opponents quite yet. When you're grateful, you play a lot better, too. This is true not just with teams but also with businesses and families. Do the work to be thankful and watch your life change.

Working at a college has a lot of benefits, including being around people who are constantly learning. There's a relationship between being thankful and growth-minded. Everyone needs to be lifelong learners. Many college coaches switch jobs often because they aren't happy with how things are where they are. I would not have been able to stay at the same school for so long if it had not been for my experience with autism and special needs. The rigors of having a child with ASD have taught me essential things in life. One of these is knowing who you work for.

I recently ran into a co-worker who was complaining about their job. They weren't being thankful, and they came across as entitled. In essence, they believed they weren't being treated fairly by the administration. If you work for a college, you work for the students, not the administration. The administration is essential, and you should play by their rules, but knowing that you work for the students is what it is all about.

This aligns with what a strong and humble carpenter told people living in an area ruled by Rome. He said to give Caesar what is Caesar's and give God what is God's. It is essential to know who you work for. Everyone needs to take time to consider who they work for. Most of the time, the answer isn't who you might think it is at first. When you know who you work for, many of your problems will disappear.

The formal academic training that colleges provide is valuable and vital. However, as important as academics are, humility and resilience are the two most important things you can learn in college.

CHAPTER 13

Coaching

P eople often tell me they have always wanted to be a coach. It seems to be one of those jobs many would like to do when they get their life in order. Coaching well is more complex than most people realize, but so are most careers. We only see the surface of what takes place, and the people part is much more complicated than it looks.

The secret about coaching is one most people know: nothing says that you need a formal team to be a coach. Nor do you need a court or a ball to coach. You become a good coach when you make your list and start doing nice things for people who cannot do anything for you. You can be a plumber, salesperson, lawyer, or electrician and be a great coach because coaching is about getting the living part of life right and giving it away.

Coaching has little to do with courts, fields, tracks, and pools, but it has everything to do with people. Of course, you need to be an expert at the craft your sport requires, but that is not the part that separates you or makes an impact. To be a good coach, you need to study your sport, but this is not what takes your team to the next level or qualifies you as a great coach.

A fantastic coach invests in people who cannot do anything for them. Most of my best coaches are not people who were coaches of sports. They were good people of various professions who took an interest in me even though I had nothing to offer them in return. One of my best coaches has autism.

I usually go to the grocery store after a long day of work. I'm almost always wearing Wofford Tennis clothes. One day, I was in the checkout line, and Sadie, the cashier, asked me, "How's Coach doing? I haven't seen him in a long time." I paused and thought, *She's talking about Mike Young.* Coach Young is Wofford's former basketball coach who's now at Virginia Tech, where he was recently named ACC Basketball Coach of the Year.

Mike has an excellent mind for basketball, but what makes him a great coach are the qualities that led me to know that Sadie was talking about him. He connects with everyone because he loves people—all people, from those who work in the checkout line to the future NBA All-Star on his basketball team. He does not love people for what they can do for him. Instead, he loves people. I'm convinced that Mike helps far more people than most know about. This makes him kind, and when we are kind, we like ourselves a lot more than when we are mean or selfish. There is evidence that Mike really enjoys coaching basketball, but he also has a lot of fun-loving people. Start taking an interest in people like Mike does, and you'll likely live a life full of joy.

The pay scale for coaches is shaped like a pyramid with a broad base at the bottom and a narrow point at the top. I'm one of those coaches whose pay is toward the bottom of the pyramid. However, I'm richer than I ever imagined. Do what matters most in life, and you will be rich, too. You might have money, and you might not. I've been surprised to learn that being rich has nothing to do with money and everything to do with relationships. I've been shown that being helpful to other people has brought me more joy than I ever knew.

Much of the New Testament is written by a guy named Paul, formerly Saul. Before he changed his name, Saul was a persecutor of early Christians. Then, he had a conversion experience and went from persecutor to follower, becoming Paul. Due to Paul's earlier life, many early Christians were reluctant to welcome him into their group. However, Barnabas persuaded them to accept Paul. Barnabas was known as "the encourager" for giving Paul a chance. He was also known to be generous with his gifts and wealth. I've been fortunate to have people in my life like Barnabas, the generous encourager. What's shocking is learning that he had a full life that had nothing to do with wealth or fame.

My wife has been my encourager. She is a wonderful person inside and out. I do not have that much to offer her. I don't have much money, nor am I good-looking, intelligent, or famous. She gives me the most fantastic gift by loving me anyway and giving love away. Despite the odds, we have an incredible life. As I mentioned previously, divorce rates for families with children with autism are much higher than the national average.

Some people believe that autism, along with other special needs, is the ultimate threat to the survival of a family. The stress can be intense. Men and women often see and feel the needs of their children differently, but when there is a disability involved, the conditions are magnified times 10 in different directions. Making objective decisions about your kids is hard, especially when a child has special needs.

Many couples argue over money. During the last financial crisis, we knew many people with marriage problems. Many of these problems were caused by financial stress. It is costly to have a child with special needs. Other couples go on vacation while you go to therapy. You are grateful for the treatment, but it doesn't seem the same.

Merritt and I knew the odds that our marriage would make it were less than average and that the chance that we would live an everyday life had been dramatically reduced. We thought we had pressure early in our marriage, but we didn't. Like many young couples, we felt pressure to achieve, buy a home, accumulate wealth, and live a good life, but having a child with ASD just about put us over the edge in the early years. To stay together, we had to adopt the mindset of a courageous, creative, and resilient dark horse. Nothing could ever be taken for granted again. We knew that we needed to communicate at a deeper level. Postponing the discussion of contentious topics was not an option we could afford.

This game was going to demand our best effort. Like the best coaches, everything we would do from this point forward would be intentional. We would make many plans, but those plans would change constantly. The competition was fierce, and it would punish us for taking the wrong shots. We had to learn that autism was something we were not going to control or fix. This was tough for two highly competitive people who believed they could work their way out of anything. We had a hard time working our way out of autism. I did not know it then, but everything would change for the better. We were in the process of receiving a gift that we knew nothing about.

We received another jab to the heart when Cole was in the first grade. The local private school he attended told us that they could no longer provide educational services for him, and we needed to find another school. We paid full price for two kids, but that did not matter. He was essentially kicked out for reasons that he had no control over. We were proud of this small school and happy he was there. Our friends had children who attended the school, and their children had not been asked to leave. We took this personally and felt that our family had been rejected. We couldn't get our minds around the idea that they did not have a place for him there.

Looking back, I know the school's decision wasn't personal. It is a great school, but its resources are limited. There is no way they can service everyone to the degree they would like. I am sure they wrestled with the decision. I missed what could have been an opportunity to lead with grace. My response demonstrated that I felt threatened. It did not show strong faith. The difficult times in our lives are the times that allow us to lead.

Since then, I still worry about my kids. Many people probably worry about their children, but I don't want to worry about them. I want to demonstrate my faith by not worrying, but sometimes, what's so close to my heart reveals my weakness. I failed the test on this occasion but learned from my mistake, as was revealed years later when Cole was lost in Washington, D.C.

Learning that I am not in charge has been a complex and beautiful education. It has also been a saving grace. This is one of the many advantages that having a child with ASD has provided me.

CHAPTER 14

Ronald McDonald

We found a new school in a nearby city that would take Cole, and it worked out great for him. It was a school for children with dyslexia. Although Cole was an avid reader who had received many diagnoses, we knew he did not have dyslexia. They must have needed students because they seemed glad to have him. We were desperate for a safe place for him to learn and grow.

Cole benefited from the one-on-one attention he received from the caring teachers and staff. The long drive to Greenville twice a day quickly got old. Since we could not figure out how to get him there and back each day, we decided to sell our house and move nearer to his new school. Merritt eventually got a job at the school, giving us a break from the costly tuition. Never in a million years did I think that I would sell my home and move to a new town because I had a child with autism.

People move for their children all the time. Autism has helped me empathize with people seeking a new country for their families. Empathy, sympathy, and pity are similar words with significantly different meanings. Empathy is understanding someone's situation and feelings from their perspective, whereas sympathy and pity come from the point of view and perspective of the person who is not going through the situation. I do not know if I would have felt the difference in these three words if it wasn't for what I thought was my biggest challenge. I was beginning to learn that a challenge can sometimes turn into a strength if you have the patience to make it through difficult times.

The move helped a lot. It was easier for our family to have a new life in Greenville and for me to commute to Wofford. Relocating was a great move, but it only solved some things. We continued to try everything we could that made sense for helping with autism.

Merritt and I believed that early intervention was necessary. She saw this firsthand in her work as a speech therapist, and I knew from athletics that it is easier to learn skills when you start young, so we were on top of it with every resource we had—and many we didn't have. We took ownership in finding a solution. We pursued music therapy, equine therapy, swimming therapy, and vision therapy. We also sought advice from renowned experts with affiliations from famous places, such as Johns Hopkins Medical Center.

I do not recommend fast food burgers and fries, but I learned a lot from eating at McDonald's every meal for an entire week. However, my experience with McDonald's restaurants differs significantly from that of most people. When I see a McDonald's, I think about our time spent in the Ronald McDonald House. The Ronald McDonald House Charities are homes supported by the famous restaurant, providing a temporary residence for families of children being treated in hospitals. RMHC now has 380 homes in 63 different countries.

One December, we had an unusually moving Christmas as we spent time in the Ronald McDonald House in Washington, D.C. The Ronald McDonald House is an incredible organization. At the RMH, we were surrounded by families whose children were very sick, including some terminally ill children. I felt young and ill-equipped to deal with the emotions I felt as I walked through the doors of the RMH.

This was an incredibly humbling experience, but we needed the help, so I was grateful to have it. During the day, we met with experts on the cutting edge of all that science and medicine had to offer. In the evenings, we would return to the respite of this wonderfully caring facility. Kind volunteers from churches and other organizations would bring meals to the families in the evening. The residents rarely made eye contact with one another out of respect because most of us were deeply hurt by our children. These were real people with real problems, and I was one of them. I felt saddened and privileged at the same time to be among them. There was a quiet and common bond that humbled me. This was another critical step in my education. I did not know it at the time, but I was learning about becoming a better coach.

My vision of the future was clouded because I had nothing to go on. I was outside of my comfort zone. From my vantage point, I had entered an aggressive ocean with high waves splashing down on my eight-foot rowboat and no land in sight. I did not know where I was going, but I was on a journey to the land of growth. If we aren't careful, our experiences can create biases about what should or should not happen.

One thing that makes autism challenging is that the diagnosis is not always precise. Children's warning signs arise with various other symptoms at different ages. The diagnosis is not always black and white like it is with some disabilities. Having a child with an invisible disability is hard. The ambiguity creates more stress and tension. We didn't want to believe anything was wrong in Cole's case. I fought it with every fiber of my body. I wasn't in denial, but I had difficulty accepting it.

As my mind circles back to that day of diagnosis, I remember thinking, *What's autism? Is that where kids are locked in their heads? How's this going to affect me?* I was growing up, but I had a long way to go. I was beginning to learn that challenging circumstances provide the best education. We left D.C. with new information and a new sense of confidence and humility, as we had met people on the cutting edge of neurological disabilities. However, we still had many questions.

CHAPTER 15

Time for a Hit

We were all hands on deck as we continued to seek the best resources to help Cole. My experience in sports has taught me that life is 10 percent what happens to you and 90 percent how you respond. Get knocked down, jump back up. Hit an obstacle, pivot, and look for new opportunities. These are themes that I not only embrace but teach daily, so I feel a lot of responsibility and desire to respond as assertively as possible.

I knew this with my mind, but I was challenged as the medical expenses grew. Cole was making progress, so there was no stopping. This was only the beginning. Money gained a new purpose, but I still wrestled with selfishness. We had financial resources, but they were limited. The supply was going to run out.

In sports, your attitude matters a lot. A *Wall Street Journal* article by James H. Hagerty in 2018 talks about how Ken Ravizza, a sports psychologist, told baseball players never to admit they were in a slump. Instead, he advised, say you're due for a hit.[31] "Attitude is a decision," said Dr. Ravizza, who taught kinesiology at California State University, Fullerton, and served as a thinking coach to the Chicago Cubs and other teams in sports ranging from rugby to water polo.

Attitude is so important that there are countless well-known sayings about attitude. Here are a few examples:

1. "Can't, never could." – Unknown

2. "You always have a choice, even if it is your attitude." – Henry Ford

3. "A bad attitude is like a flat tire; you won't get anywhere until you change it." – Unknown

4. "The worst disability in life is a bad attitude." – Dale Carnegie.

This list could go on and on. You can name many of your own that you may have learned from an influential parent, teacher, or mentor. Statements about attitude are easy to think about when things are going well. Motivation matters a lot, too, as it takes a lot of incentive to push forward when things are not going well. In these times, drawing upon the forces of a good attitude takes much inspiration. Having a great attitude can become a habit over time, just like having a bad attitude can. Knowing this is very important to not let the dangers of having a lousy attitude sneak up on you.

Staying highly motivated is also a habit. Great athletes sometimes lose their motivation. This usually comes from being discouraged. Being highly motivated takes work. It helps to be around others with high levels of motivation who are willing to encourage you.

Champions adapt and overcome. The Big Coach of Life had called my name for the starting lineup in a game. This would take every ounce of perseverance and courage that I could find. I began asking for help from a power I couldn't see or describe.

How we respond in storms speaks the truth about what we believe. My belief was shallow, and what I valued wasn't much better. A transformation happened to me. Cole's diagnosis was the catalyst for change. This was personal, profound, and frightening. As I look back, I realize that change always happens in such moments. I haven't seen change in my life when the seas were smooth.

Think about those times in your life when you grew up the most. Consider the circumstances and environment. Chances are, the times when you grew the most were also the times when you had the least control. Being uncomfortable is paramount for becoming the person you were intended to be. We see this in sports a lot. Players or teams that make us uncomfortable cause us to grow the most.

I feel very fortunate that for the last ten years, our team has been able to play the University of North Carolina, which is often one of the top teams in the country. The growth begins when we step out of the van into a sea of blue, leading us into one of the premier facilities in the country to play a team with the best recruits who are very well-coached. This is a growth experience that we look forward to attacking. When we get to choose a difficult or easy schedule, choosing hard is always good.

Some people make a change because their life has hit rock bottom, and they begin to consider that their life has nowhere to go but up. Others create change because they gain knowledge that something better is out there for them to go after. Change requires a catalyst to get the engine of growth moving. When we undergo enough change and receive the proper coaching, we can learn to trust and embrace change as a necessity for living a whole life.

I don't believe in coincidence. When I look back on significant events in my life, it is easy to see that things happen for a reason. There is a plan, and everyone's plan is different, and so are the reasons for the changes in my life. Once I understood this, life began to make a lot more sense. This growth in understanding gives us confidence, knowing that we're part of a plan.

When I received the gut-punch diagnosis of my son's autism, although I didn't realize it then, I was not living my life to the best of my ability. I had a beautiful wife, a lovely home, money in the bank, and the job of my dreams. My charmed situation was not helping my cause. There was no reason for me to make a change on the outside. The opposite was happening.

I had been using my charmed life to hope my magical life would continue. I was pursuing a life of ease and comfort. Sure, I wanted to be successful, but that was it. Success was covered with a selfish motive. This is no way to live; it is the opposite of boldness and courage.

CHAPTER 16

No Choice but to Forgive

When Cole was in the sixth grade, he went on a four-day field trip with his class to New York City and Washington, D.C. I was ecstatic that he could go, and we smiled as the bus departed South Carolina and headed off for four days of experiencing history and culture in two of our nation's most exciting cities.

Everything was perfect, and then, three days into the trip, I got a call while I was with my team at practice that would become a pivotal moment. Ironically, I never answer my phone when I'm at practice, but on this day, I did.

When I looked down at the phone, I recognized it was Ms. A.J., one of Cole's school administrators. When I answered, she said, "Rod, I'm so sorry, but I want you to know that we're in downtown Washington and cannot find Cole. We are looking everywhere."

I said, "Don't worry, I know you'll find him. Take a deep breath. Everything will be OK. Just let me know when you find him." At that point, I was cool under pressure. A strange calm came over me as an inner voice told me how I interacted with Ms. A.J. was important. After reassuring her again, I hung up the phone and told the team that if I got another call, I'd need to take it.

A few minutes went by before the phone rang again. This time, I did not recognize the number, but I answered anyway to hear a voice say, "Mr. Ray, this is Captain Brown with the D.C. Police Department. I want you to know that we are doing everything possible to find your son, but I need your help answering a few questions."

He wanted to know how Cole might respond to different situations. The police were also trying to find clues about who might have lured him away from the group. I needed to maintain self-discipline to help them. As he explained their process of securing the area around the National Mall and the monuments, I stayed calm. I knew that being thoughtful and calm was paramount to providing helpful information.

There would be additional calls from the police and officers from our national park security office. I explained the situation to my team as tears rolled down my cheeks. The team didn't know what to say or how to respond. This sort of thing doesn't happen every day at tennis practice.

According to the non-profit autism awareness organization Autism Speaks, a new study in the journal *Pediatrics* found that of 1,218 parents surveyed with children with ASD, 49 percent reported that their children participated in wandering. Of those wanderings, 53 percent were long enough to cause worry, 65 percent involved a close call with traffic, and 24 percent involved a close call with drowning.[32]

Parenting is a stressful endeavor. If you've forgotten and need a reminder, watch parents' behavior at their children's sporting events or performances. Watch them sit alone, scream at the officials, talk awkwardly with others, and more. Then, add in the elements of a special needs child, such as autism, and you can see why the stress level rises above what's on any chart. Losing a child with autism who has wandered away is enough to put any normal person over the edge because you're already on edge from the daily challenges that go with taking care of that child.

Cole had been lost before. One time, he had gotten lost in a park near our house, and another time, near my parents' home in North Carolina. He had been lost countless times at the grocery store and other local places, and every time, I'd worry about finding him, but I'd also worry about the onslaught of negative attention that would be directed our way. However, this time, it was different. Washington, D.C., was a seven-hour drive away.

I felt helpless. For a moment, I imagined driving to Washington and single-handedly shutting down our nation's capital. A few deep breaths and some positive visualization of Cole being found helped me gain a clearer perspective that this event was outside my control.

Explaining the situation to Merritt on the phone was a challenge. I felt that my tone of voice and positive attitude that he would soon be found was important. I had been given the chance to be a leader and was determined to execute it well. We were in this together. We were both calm, but we were a mess.

A few hours passed, and I got a call that Cole had been found in the Smithsonian Museum. He had somehow gotten separated from the group in a rainstorm. He was fine, and we were thrilled that he had been found.

The story about Cole being lost traveled fast in our tight-net community. Principals and school administrators called us to apologize. We were never angry, nor did we pass blame. Plain and simple, we were always thankful that our child had been found. Ms. A.J. remained a well-respected and admired friend.

Autism has taught me to have empathy and concern for others in a way that I did not before. This has made me humbler and more resilient. I still have a long way to go in this area, but I'm more willing to change than I've ever been.

CHAPTER 17

Purpose

I believe there's a purpose for my life beyond the one that I'm comfortable living. Greatness isn't attained by playing it safe. Greatness comes from taking risks, working hard, being creative, and having a purpose greater than our material world. I want to focus more on helping other people than accumulating more comfort. The answer to happiness is quite simple, but it does not mean happiness is easy. I can be fooled into thinking that easy, comfortable, happy, and fulfilled go together, but they do not. Life doesn't work that way because there is so much more to it.

Sometimes, I don't have the courage or ambition to focus on helping others. This is why I must be more intentional about it as a goal, just like the goal of exercising, reading more, getting more sleep, or anything else worth doing. The people I surround myself with influence me, guiding my thoughts and ambitions.

I have never sincerely asked to be in a place where I see the world differently than before. This is a new and ongoing opportunity and dilemma. Autism has been the worst thing that ever happened to me, and it has been the best. Bitter or better, I received a graduate degree in how life can change for the good in an uncomfortable place.

My attitude matters a lot. When I'm humble, I'm at my best. Arrogance is the opposite of humility. Arrogant players are a recipe for disaster. They hurt team chemistry, and arrogance prevents them from consistently competing at their best. An arrogant player will not reach their potential. Arrogant players fear making mistakes, so they don't compete freely. When the game is on the line, I want someone in the match who does not fear making mistakes. The ego's effect on an arrogant player carries too much weight, which ultimately causes them to cave under pressure.

Confidence, arrogance, and ego do not have a healthy relationship with one another. Confidence helps us accomplish great things for good, but arrogant and egotistical players are dangerous. I don't know many people with special needs who are arrogant, but many possess confidence. Gaining confidence, as with many good things, often takes time. Sometimes, the best education is found in the school of hard knocks. Many people with special needs are humble and confident and do not allow their focus to dwell on their weaknesses.

Sports commentators often talk about the underdog, and some fans like to pull for the Cinderella story, but it is different when you have a disadvantage as a way of life. Learning to live an extraordinary life with a disadvantage makes you a superhero. It is no coincidence that many people with autism are attracted to superheroes.

We have learned much about autism recently, but it is still a relatively new disease without a known cause or perfect treatment. Educators, healthcare professionals, and neighbors are still learning. This is precisely what makes the disorder so challenging. No one knows how to treat people with autism, so we often ignore them.

I've learned that asking hard questions is better than ignoring people. Instead of avoiding someone difficult, I've learned to speak to them and try to see them where they are. I've learned the importance of the pursuit of empathy, even though I might not get it right. When we ignore people, we treat them like second-class citizens instead of like equals.

Knowing that the only thing constant is change sounds good in theory. It supports the idea that we all would like to have a growth mindset. But look around—how many people do you know who are actually looking for a change? I can easily list how I want other people to change. But let's be honest, how many of us are looking for a change because we know it is good for us? If we stay comfortable, change is acceptable, but what about being uncomfortable? We can't grow when relaxed, but we seek ease and comfort. Growth happens when we are uncomfortable. Do you believe this to be true? We believe it, but we don't pursue these opportunities.

Since we receive growth opportunities without asking, they are gifts. They are not, however, gifts in the usual sense, like the ones we give each other on special occasions. Those gifts are often forgotten within the year. The gifts I am talking about are those that penetrate us enough to create change. Autism was a gift. I did not know it at the time of my child's diagnosis, but it is now clear to me that it was a gift.

Almost everything has changed for the better. This is a common theme that keeps shining through. Since my brokenness, almost everything has changed for the better. I believe that I was scooped up and carried to a better place. Some people might call this faith. I'm not sure what I call it, but I know I'm glad it happened, and I hope it will happen to many other people, too. I'm not glad for autism, but I'm glad for the transformation that has occurred because of difficulty. It isn't just difficulty, though. I think it goes much further than difficulty. We can do hard things, such as run a race up a mountain, but they will quickly bring satisfaction.

Henri Nouwen, one of the most-read Christian writers of the last century and author of 42 books, wrote about pain and loss. Pain is a better way to describe the sorrow that can make life rich. In *Bread for the Journey*, Henri Nouwen remarks:

> Every time we decide to love someone, we open ourselves to great suffering because those we most love cause us great joy and pain. The greatest pain comes from leaving ... the pain of leaving can tear us apart.

> Still, if we want to avoid the suffering of leaving, we will never experience the joy of loving. And love is stronger than fear, life stronger than death, hope stronger than despair. We must trust that the risk of loving is always worth taking.

There's a fascinating relationship between pain, love, loss, and joy. Pain can take us places that we can't go without it. We need pain if we're going to have a full life, yet when I'm in the throes of pain, I try to avoid it. When I reflect on times of pain, I can see that most pain does have a relationship with joy.

I can understand the relationship between pain and joy when I apply it to sports. Usually, you won't experience the joy that comes from success if you don't first endure the pain that comes from hard work and loss. In sports, a team might sacrifice and still not win, so we must change the way we think about the pain of regret. Work hard and give everything you have, and you'll have fewer regrets.

Living a life without regrets is a goal worth pursuing. I'm not speaking about not making mistakes in general because everyone makes mistakes, and we can look back and think how we could have handled a situation differently. Regret is more along the lines of asking yourself, *Did I try hard? How am I living today? Is there an area in my life that I need to clean up now?* This way of thinking keeps you in the present, which keeps the focus off of the loss of what could have been. This is also a great reference point when you're faced with decisions. Which choice is more likely to cause regret?

I need to stay closer to the idea that when one door closes, another door opens. This keeps me closer to being growth-minded and focused on the future rather than the past. This mindset is in line with control of the controllables. Both are important in sports, business, relationships, and life with a loved one with autism.

I've had the privilege of writing many letters of recommendation for former players. These are typically meaningful letters because I can speak from the heart about how much I've seen the players grow, overcome difficulty, and persevere. College is a great space for growing in character. In many cases, I get to speak with recruiters or managers searching for employees, which is fun because, over the years, I've become so invested in the players. Employers want to work with high-character people who persevere, so if I can get on the phone with them, my players are an easy sell.

Time and time again, I hear from people who say they like hiring athletes. They never say this because athletes have had it easy. It is always because they appreciate that the student-athlete has had to overcome difficulty under pressure.

People who succeed fail more than people who don't. Just because we fail, it doesn't mean we have regrets. Failure is okay. I don't want to regret how I respond to failure.

CHAPTER 18

Keep Coming Back

The opportunity to impact lives as a college coach is remarkable. Coaches spend more time with students than any other adults on the college campus. This is an important responsibility that coaches need to consider. I see it as a huge responsibility and sometimes even feel it as a heavy burden I need to get right. I know that even the best coaches with great intentions are going to make a lot of mistakes. Ironically, the college coaches I admire don't see themselves as the best coaches. They're very intentional about taking care of their players, but I don't think they overthink how good they are at coaching because that's what coaching is.

Due to the competitive nature of college sports, conflicts will arise, and there will inevitably be hurt feelings over playing time, performance, and decisions made away from the game. College is an excellent time in young people's lives. College is centered around the critical formal education of learning, but humility and resiliency can be the best things to learn in college. These are not easy things to know, which is what makes college coaching so essential and challenging.

So, if I teach humility and resiliency, I need to be humble and resilient personally and professionally. I've learned the hard way that I can't be resilient unless I'm humble. By definition, a humble person is someone who isn't proud—somebody who is modest. To me, this means that I should put other people first. It isn't easy for me to be modest or lead my family in a modest way because I want the best for them. Now I realize that I should want the best for everyone.

Coaching at the smallest NCAA Division I school is not for the faint of heart. We're the dark horse every day, but our mindset is strong. Wofford's mascot, a Boston Terrier, suits us well as a tough little short-haired dog. One of my favorite sayings is to make the big time where you are. This should go for all of us no matter where we are.

Never think, *I'd be a better coach/player/student if I were at a bigger school.* This type of thinking is a trap. Always make the big time where you are! Here are some examples of faulty thinking, followed by a more positive way of looking at the situation:

1. I'd be nicer if people were nicer to me. Be nice anyway.

2. I'd be a better stockbroker if I worked on Wall Street. Be the best you can be where you are. Do the little things better than anyone else, and think big.

3. I'd be a better wife or husband if my spouse treated me better. Treat them better and see what happens.

4. I'd be a better teammate if my teammates were all in. Be a great teammate and see what happens.

This list could go on and on. Not treating our situation like it is big time is nothing but an excuse.

The above thought process is a version of the "Paradoxical Commandments." They gained great notoriety because Mother Teresa hung a poster with them listed on the wall of her school in Calcutta for inspiration. They have also been called the "Anyway Poem." Dr. Kent Keith wrote them.[33] The words of the actual charter are listed below:

People are often unreasonable, illogical, and self-centered.
Forgive them anyway.

If you are kind, people may accuse you of selfish, ulterior motives.
Be kind anyway.

If you are successful, you will win some false friends and some true enemies.
Succeed anyway.

If you are honest, people may cheat you.
Be honest anyway.

What you spend years building, someone could destroy overnight.
Build anyway.

If you find serenity and happiness, they may be jealous.
Be happy anyway.

The good you do today, people will often forget tomorrow.
Do good anyway.

Give the world the best you have, and it may never be enough.
Give the world the best you've got anyway.

You see, in the final analysis, it is between you and your God.
It was never between you and them anyway.

I'd like to know what inspired Mother Teressa to hang the "Anyway Poem" on her wall. She worked with the most marginalized people in the world. Her clients were the poorest of children, the sick, and the dying. Many had little hope beyond their next glass of water. I guess Mother Teressa wasn't one to make excuses because she believed her work was of the utmost importance. The "Paradoxical Commandments" most likely spoke to her.

College coaches who make excuses don't fare very well. Neither do small business owners—or anyone else taking a chance or putting themselves out there. Mother Teressa was taking a chance on the poor and couldn't afford to lose. This is how it should be everywhere, especially when we have the privilege of potentially helping other people.

Let's return to the top of the list: "People are often unreasonable, illogical, and self-centered. Forgive them anyway." Understanding this statement alone is more than enough for me in one sitting. I'm analytical and detail-oriented. Educationally, I have an M.B.A., which is primarily a quantitative study of how things can and should work best. Therefore, forgiving people who are unreasonable, illogical, and self-centered doesn't make any sense to me. Forgiveness is a complicated place to start. It helps me to begin with the word "tolerate." For example, people will be irrational. Tolerating them is much easier than forgiving them.

However, forgiveness goes much beyond mere tolerance in obtaining a pure heart. I need to be tolerant, but tolerance and acceptance don't get the job done. Forgiveness is the answer and the key. Mother Teressa must have known this. The marginalized people who were her clients had been neglected by their society and country. She knew this, but she couldn't get hung up on it if she was to provide the needed help. It is fair to say that very few people could meet her standards, but she loved them anyway. This is a powerful way to live. The poem could have been named the "Powerful Poem." I believe we become bulletproof when we learn to live this way.

Most people get into college coaching for two reasons: love of competition and the relationships they build. However, the job is challenging. Players struggle, and the stakes are high. The market doesn't wait for quarterly profits. Results are posted weekly, and people will let you down.

The guys I coach are top-notch. Intelligent, athletic, and hardworking. One-on-one sports, like tennis, attract super-competitive people; our players are no exception. They compete against fierce competitors, too. These excellent tennis players have made a massive commitment to reach this level.

Many people are competing for a finite number of scholarships and playing opportunities. Win and advance. Lose and go home. Do this over and over again.

Thousands of 12-year-olds dream of becoming professional tennis players. The path to the top is brutal. The road to college tennis is also long and arduous. Learning to lose is a big piece of becoming great. The best players learn to recover from the loss quickly, not wasting time being stuck. Hating to lose while being good at recuperating from failure is necessary for a player to reach their potential. Most people dislike losing, but the most competitive people despise losing in the most extreme way.

There's often a discussion as to whether it is best for a player to love to play because they love winning or if the best players win because they hate losing so much. The best players are highly competitive, engaged, and emotionally disciplined people willing to push through more than their fair share of pain and adversity to become the best they can be.

Many good athletes become disillusioned with losing and quit prematurely, but it does not have to be this way. Players with high self-esteem can weather losses with the proper support and coaching. The term that is often used to describe this state is "burnout." Failing to deal with stress and pressure over a prolonged period causes burnout.

People in real life outside of sports also face burnout, but they, too, can avoid it. Staying competitive while learning to lose is living life to the fullest. When it comes to overcoming my own losses, I've memorized the steps below so I have them to draw upon.

1. I do not know if losing is good or bad. Just because it feels terrible at the time, it does not mean it is necessarily bad. Stay in the moment and focus on what is before you without projecting.

2.   Obstacles and disappointment make me better. I'm in a relationship with the competition. We need each other, so I welcome challenging circumstances as tools to help me grow. Competition can come in many forms. Sometimes, it is outside of me. Most of the time, it is inside of me.

3.   The only way to flourish and become my best is to regularly face uncomfortable moments. Learn to cherish them.

When losing happens, we don't know if it is good or bad because we cannot see the future. Much good can come from difficult situations. We might not realize it when the loss occurs, but later, we sometimes look back and see the good. For example, we've all had friends who lose their jobs only to find themselves happier and more helpful in another career or pursuit. This happens in coaching a lot. Some people are great assistant coaches but terrible head coaches, and vice versa. I've also seen it with players who reinvent themselves after losing starting positions.

I'm reminded of the essay "Welcome to Holland" by Emily Perl Kingsley.[34] The essay describes the experience of raising a child with a disability. Kingsley writes about a couple who planned a trip to Rome to see the roses. They had saved for this trip and prepared for a long time. Every detail was planned out perfectly. They boarded the plane, and the flight was fine. However, when the plane landed, the captain announced, "Welcome to Holland."

All their lives, they had dreamed of going to Rome, but the plane had landed in Holland, and there was no way to get to Rome from there. They were stuck in their new destination. At first, they thought their trip was a disaster until they discovered that the tulips in Holland were just as beautiful as the roses in Italy, and Holland had windmills and Rembrandts. The couple was a long way from Rome, but they learned to have a great appreciation for all that Holland had to offer. This is how we should deal with people, especially people with special needs.

I learned that wishing things were different is a waste of time. What's that going to do? I might miss the beauty of the tulips because I was frustrated that they weren't roses. I've learned to love tulips. In fact, they are my favorite flower.

The players I recruit never turn out how I thought they would while I was recruiting them. Many overachieve, while just as many underachieve. Many whom I thought were extroverts turned out to be introverts. They always turn out differently than I thought they would. Even if I believe someone will be a particular player, their college experience never follows a straight line. They may be an incredible athlete who is confident and has a track record of success. This does not guarantee that they will not have people problems—quite the contrary. In my experience, there will always be "people problems." The exciting part is that "people problems" are not problems but tools for college student-athletes to learn from. This is precisely how it is supposed to work.

Earlier today, our team had its first team meeting of the year. We have some outstanding freshmen, but to be honest, I do not know what kind of year they will have—or what type of season anyone on the team will have, for that matter. Coaches try to make recruiting a science, and some get very good at it, but there is too much to learn about people in the recruiting process.

Rob Galloway, one of our former players, is currently playing the highest level of professional tennis and plays in top-level tournaments such as the US Open and Wimbledon. When I recruited him, I had no idea he would play in three US Opens and be ranked 42nd in the world (he will likely be much higher by the time you read this). If I had known, would I have treated him differently than I did eight years ago when he was a freshman? Of course, I would have, but I'm not sure it would have helped him.

It would be less exciting or fun if I could control how the players turn out. Coaching would be boring. The same is true in the world outside of sports. If I go to work expecting people to be a certain way, I'm going to be highly disappointed, but if I go to work knowing that I'm going to be surrounded by God's kids who are going to act like kids, I'm going to have a whole lot more fun. This is very important for me to embrace and demonstrate to others. When I show a spirit that allows mistakes, everyone is happier, including myself. There is just no way that perfection is the goal because, in perfection, there is no freedom.

Obstacles and disappointment make us better. Have you spent time around a spoiled child, a kid who seems to have everything and has not faced much disappointment? That situation only sometimes turns out well when it comes to character. What makes us think that we are any different? We are not. It just does not work that way. When it comes to character, we need obstacles and adversity to help us become the people we would like to be.

The way to grow is to regularly make yourself uncomfortable. "Rough seas make a skillful sailor" is a popular and well-known saying. Everyone who sails would like to be a good sailor. Everyone who lives would like to live a good life, so let's not run from the rough times because they are precisely what help us become who we are intended to be. These lessons teach you to see life's challenges as opportunities rather than threats. This is an important step not only in sports but in life.

Making it as a professional tennis player is difficult because you are usually an independent contractor for many years. You pay your bills, like many people starting a business. The pay scale is top-loaded, so the stars make most of the money. Since the professional route is so difficult, most of the best players in the world pursue college tennis. This makes the level of college play incredibly high. For example, it typically takes 10 years of year-round training to be a good college player. The commitment required is incredible. Most burn out, become frustrated, lose their edge, run out of money, and quit. The players who make it have faced adversity many, many times. This is what makes succeeding at the professional level so fantastic—the difficulty makes the success meaningful.

I believe disadvantages can be turned into advantages when extra effort is the norm. Creativity is necessary to survive. Roadblocks exist at every turn, so I expect them. However, I better not let them define me. Coaching at this level for over 20 years has taught me how to fight and overcome difficulties. Nothing is easy. I wouldn't trade anything for this experience.

Coaches spend a lot of time recruiting players because we won't keep our jobs if we don't have good players. When I go to a high-level tournament to recruit, I'm often asked if I see anyone I like, as if the smallest school in the country will tag someone and take them home. *See anyone I like?* I'm recruiting good players who are getting attention from many good programs.

One of the most important parts of recruiting good players is connecting with them. There are approximately 275 schools in the country with Division I teams, plus another nearly 500 Division II or III. Therefore, a good player has a lot of wonderful options. This makes recruiting very competitive. Since there are so many good schools, coaches must find a way to relate with prospects early in the process. One of the best ways to connect is to ask the prospect to talk about the adversity they have faced.

Try this exercise about dealing with adversity. First, consider the troubles you have dealt with in your life. Next, name three challenging things. Then please take a few minutes to write one of them down and describe it in four sentences. It could be something you worked through, or it could be something that you are still dealing with today. Either way, the chances are excellent that it made an impression on you and shaped you into who you are today. In other words, without its influence, you would likely be a different person. Are you a better or worse person because of your difficulty?

Just like you, the people I recruit are better because of the challenges they've faced. Their difficulties include the illness of a family member, financial hardship, parents getting divorced, substance abuse, injury, and many others. Getting to the point in a recruiting relationship where these types of struggles are shared is central to building a relationship that will grow. It is necessary to have a real relationship that will continue to develop.

It takes a lot to put together a great team. If you have a great team or business, you must have a well-thought-out plan. Logistics, product knowledge, finances, and every detail must be covered. These areas are essential, but everyone has them, so they are necessary to win. If you want to win, you must have great relationships, too. Super Bowl-winning teams have winning chemistry.

In Division I sports, every team has excellent facilities. It has become a facility race. As soon as someone builds a new facility, the race is on, and the next thing you know, everyone else is making something better. As a result, athletic facilities today are much nicer than 20 years ago. While amenities that go with gyms and stadiums are incredible, if you don't have great relationships, you will not produce a great team. Without great relationships, all the effort put into building exceptional facilities is wasted.

Relationships are with people, and people have people problems. We are not robots; our wheels will come off the tracks. We all have wheelbases of different widths, but when we try to drive in the same way on the same tracks, it isn't an exact fit and doesn't work out the same for everyone. Things are only sometimes going to work out perfectly, and this is what creates our challenges.

Ironically, it is our differences that make us so enjoyable. When we miss learning about one another's challenges, we miss out on one of the essential parts of being human. I learned this from autism, and it has made me a better coach. I have faced other challenges, too, that have led to growth.

There's also nothing to discuss when there's no fight or struggle. For example, as a teenager, I did not handle a move that my family made very well. Indeed, I could have dealt with this much better, but that is not the point. The point is that the move made me more understanding of others who are outside of their comfort zone.

On the outside, I looked like I was doing fine, but I was struggling on the inside. This helped me understand that the same might be true for other people. This was a lesson I needed to learn. The timing was terrible, but it, too, was an instrumental part of the struggle. Since then, I've learned to embrace struggle because I have seen how good things come from struggle. I've been blessed to coach players from all over the world who have come to our team. My struggle to adjust to the move as a teenager has undoubtedly helped me empathize with the players I've coached.

Empathy can breed and lead to more empathy, which makes life more fun. The struggle is the beginning of everything good. I do not believe that we're born knowing this, but it is central to living a happy life because it helps us keep the challenges we face in the correct perspective.

CHAPTER 19

Seek Difficulty

Successfully navigating life with a disability makes a short list of hard things. Some people do not know what to do with people with disabilities. If we take the time to get to know someone who is not like us, we will see they are just like other people, but it takes commitment, knowledge, and understanding to get to that point.

Many people with disabilities have a hard time with employment. This is true with people on the autism spectrum, too. They may have social challenges, making it difficult to connect with coworkers and employers. Consequently, it is believed that 80 percent of college graduates with autism are unemployed or underemployed.

Learning that college graduates with autism struggle to find meaningful employment impacted me. It gave me insight into the importance of personal relationships in the workforce. It also taught me that we need to find a way to get many more people involved in helping with this challenge. As I began to explore this challenge with others at my college and friends of mine in business, my curiosity grew. I believed the situation did not have to be this way, so I started talking more about it.

One day, I got a call from Michelle, whom I had never met. Michelle cleaned houses in a city about 35 miles away to make extra money. She told me she had gotten my name from a friend whose house she cleaned. She began telling me about her nephew Tyler, who was visually impaired. Tyler is a bright and good-looking college graduate who had unsuccessfully searched for a job for five years. She told me she believed I could help him find a job.

Remarkable! I remember thinking, *Tyler doesn't drive, lives in another town, and believes I can find him a job. I'm a tennis coach. How in the world am I going to do this? Aren't there other people more qualified than me to help him? People who work in the employment industry, own companies, or at least have experience with the visually impaired? I'm hardly qualified.* Then I realized I had something significant: compassion.

My son's autism has given me the gift of compassion, and it is up to me to use it in every positive way possible. That was a big moment for me. I went to work helping Tyler and Michelle. I met Tyler and his service dog, Shadow, for coffee. We became friends, and I became more invested.

I started by asking everyone I knew if they could think of anyone who could help Tyler. I was surprised by the number of people who showed interest, but I couldn't think of how they might help. I persisted and wasn't afraid to ask. One day, a friend contacted me to say he had an opening in his real estate office and was interested in speaking with Tyler. I explained that if he hired Tyler, it could change the whole chemistry of his company. This man was a very successful real estate investor, but I told him that hiring Tyler would be the best investment he would ever make. It worked. Tyler now has a great job, his company loves him, and Shadow is the firm's full-time mascot.

I now have relationships with other young men with special needs, and they help me in so many ways. My life is richer when I'm willing to be helpful. People like Tyler are humble, courageous, and resilient. These are not easy qualities to attain as they come with a cost, but I've come to believe that learning them is living. I'm happier with my living a lot more than I am when the stock market rises.

I'm happier than ever today because I'm less burdened with the heavy weight of my selfishness. I believe most people want to be satisfied. Have you ever wondered how happy you'd like to be? A little happy or super delighted? True happiness comes with a cost: you must put the lives and agendas of others (who can do nothing for you) ahead of your own. Some people learn this early on, and others, like me, learn it later in life.

Athletes have the most fun playing for their team or something bigger than themselves. Tennis is typically an individual sport, but college tennis is a team sport. Most players who come to me need more experience being part of a team. Guess what? The vast majority love playing for a team because it shifts the focus from me-centric to team-centric. However, many teams have players who could be happier. This is usually because they still operate like individuals, so they miss some of the best parts of being on a team.

I know a player who left an excellent college team to play for another school. He soon realized that most of his teammates didn't care if he left. He thought everyone was out for themselves at the highest level of college sports. I do not believe this to be true of every team. I've seen firsthand where the player on the bench is cheering for the person who took their spot. Although it is not always this way, this is how a great team is supposed to be. The takeaway is that this is how we are also supposed to live. Cheer for someone who has more than you; you can't go wrong.

I have a friend named Robb whose thoughts and experiences have taught me much. When Robb's boss was retiring, Robb was next in line to be the director of an organization he had served for over 25 years. As Robb prepared to compete for the position, he knew a national search would be conducted. Robb wanted the job but respected the necessary process so the right person could be hired in good conscience. As the interviewing process began to unfold, Robb realized that many top-notch candidates were pursuing the job he had worked hard for, one that many believed was rightfully his. He cared about the people around him and thought he was the right person to lead the organization in a way that would best serve others.

I remember the day he humbly told me that he wanted the job but he would be the best employee his new boss ever had if he did not get it. I was stunned, but he was sincere. If he was not hired as the director, the next best job was the one he currently held, and an essential part of that position was to support the director. Robb had made up his mind. He was going to be happy either way.

Leadership is not a title. Leadership is a mindset. If Robb did not get the position, he could lead by serving the person who got the job he wanted. People with disabilities have no choice but to live this way. They constantly deal with handicaps outside their control—playing the "why me" game is the biggest threat to their happiness. I see this happen with college athletes as well. It happens everywhere. We have a choice to make. Are we going to live a life where we pull for everyone?

In a recent college football game, the field goal kicker missed two relatively routine kicks in a row at the end of the fourth quarter while the game was tied. As he entered the game for his third attempt in a matter of minutes, I couldn't help but wonder what the backup kicker was thinking. Was every player on the team holding their breath, hoping their kicker would knock it dead, while the backup kicker secretly hoping they'd miss? If so, that would be very sad. We have all felt this way at one time or another, but we must guard against it. When we react this way, we need to understand what the cause is. Only then can we make peace with ourselves and begin to put the other person first.

A wise young carpenter had a group of followers approximately two thousand years ago. He told his friends to pray for their enemies. I've offered the same advice to my players. I don't know if it helps their opponents, but I'm certain it benefits them.

I learned this the hard way. Autism and coaching at the smallest Division I school in the country taught me this. If I had not learned this lesson, there is just no way I could have been happy. It all boils down to being able to cheer for the person who took your spot on the team or who has a better team.

Early in my career, we were playing against one of our local rivals, Furman University, coached at the time by the legendary Paul Scarpa, the winningest Division I college coach in the country. Paul was a fantastic coach, and it was no accident that his teams won a lot. That day, we got off to a great start in front of a packed home crowd. The energy was electric, and everything went our way until the momentum shifted. Furman came back and won a terrifically close match.

As I shook hands with the great coach, he looked me dead in the eye and said, "Sorry, Rod. You had us today. I thought you were going to win." Paul is one of the most competitive people I've ever met, and yet he was sorry that our team had lost that day. A part of him had been pulling for an upset. Of course, he wanted his team to win, but he wanted our team to win, too.

I gained much respect for him that day. He understood the importance of wanting everyone to succeed. This is one of the reasons he was a great coach. Remember, you don't need to coach a sport to be great. Pull for everyone; it will make you better. I believe this is one of the reasons that the famous humble carpenter told us to pray for our enemies. I don't know if it helps the enemy, but I'm convinced it helps the one pulling for the competition.

I have so many awesome friends in the coaching arena. These are competitive people who wake up in the middle of the night after a tough loss or difficult situation. These people want to win more than they want to breathe, but what makes them unique is that they want the other guy to be happy and successful, too.

As a coach, I am responsible for demonstrating this attitude to my players. Not only does it make me a better person, but it dramatically helps them, too. This attitude has transformed the way that I live. Fundamentally, I think many people who go into coaching college tennis live like this. Most of us have had to be willing to work very hard for low wages. To be happy in this role, I have had to develop the heart of a servant.

The score is important in sports. Coaches who lose a lot get fired, and players who lose a lot sit on the bench. Winning involves real money and opportunity in college sports, but the score is only one way to define winning. Winning only on the score is not sustainable for the long term. It is best to succeed in the score category and in all the other ways that matter, too, but this isn't how it works. I've learned that I need to win in critical ways first.

One thing that makes autism challenging is that it doesn't always show at birth. For instance, my son was already attending school when we learned he needed testing. Some people do not know what to do with children with neurological disabilities. I believe that having a child with a disability has helped me to see every person as one of God's kids. This mind shift hit me loud and clear. One of our most important jobs in life is to take care of God's kids. Believing in a higher power has been important to me. Living in a way that demonstrates this belief is also significant.

I've looked at disabled people with eyes that inwardly scream, "Thank God that isn't my child or me." This says more about me than the other person. Does feeling this way mean that I don't think I could handle it? Or is it more of a selfish motive that says that that person's disability might get in the way of what I want? When I think this way, I'm essentially playing God because I don't know if it would be good or bad in the big picture.

Autism is a disability that can cause social and behavioral challenges in a world where the ability to build personal relationships opens doors; folks with autism have high mountains to climb. They get left out of many group events because they don't navigate the people part well. This is an area where awareness creates more understanding and inclusiveness of people who do not act like our other friends.

I receive hundreds of letters recommending I look at a particular player because a coach or family member thinks they are a good fit for our team. They will often use the word "potential" to describe the prospect.

I've learned to be careful of players with the potential tag. We never reach our potential, so why is this prospect with potential so far under the recruiting radar? What has held them back, and what are they waiting for? There might be a good reason, but the defense shouldn't be a lack of initiative or bad character. They might be underdeveloped because they had complicated injuries, grew too fast, or played in a league where their competition was so bad that they weren't seen. I'm looking for that player who is under the radar of what most coaches are looking for. This doesn't happen much today, yet the letters about high potential keep arriving in my inbox.

Send me a note explaining that the prospect is a great athlete with incredible drive and determination, and I'll be interested. It isn't that complicated. We can all see where we have missed out on opportunities. I realize this is important because it can be a catalyst for changing the future. It starts with how we do the little things. It is never too late or too early to become better.

People who realize there is urgency in living a whole life get more done, make more friends, and have a more significant impact. These people attack the day and go after their opportunities. They live as if their days are numbered. They do not fear death but, instead, go after possibilities. The people who knock on the door of "being all they came to be" typically do it in many areas of their lives—thus, the saying, "How you do anything is how you do everything."

Potential is not it. Drive and determination work in the long run. The only place where success comes before work is in the dictionary. I cannot tell you how many unsuccessful but talented players I see while recruiting. The sooner a person begins working hard, the more adept they will appear later.

Of course, ability, talent, and aptitude are some predictors of how high we go, but they are not in total control. Other factors are just as important and should be taken seriously. For example, let's say person A has an ability level of 12 but only reaches 60 percent of their capacity. They will have a production ratio of 7.2. On the other hand, person B has an ability level of 11 but reaches 70 percent of their capacity; they will have a production ratio of 7.7. In addition, person B will significantly impact other factors such as team chemistry, loyalty, consistency, and dependability.

The best gift I can give a player is to demonstrate to them that I know with all my heart that they are great. When I was young, I had a coach who told me he'd rather have a player like me, who was hard-working, than someone talented. Up until that point, I'd believed I had a gift. He tried to pay me the ultimate compliment, but I missed it. However, I've learned not to make that statement to others or myself. Never let anyone tell you that talent is the factor because it is not. You cannot control your ability, but you can control what you do with your ability, and there is always room for improvement.

I sometimes stress about governments, employers, and family members when my most significant opportunity for improvement lies within me. I want to focus on reaching my unmet potential instead of trying to fix things that I can't—something I still often try to do. Call me stubborn, call me crazy, but learn from me. I'm currently saving pain and aggravation from not trying to fix others. I think this makes them a lot happier, too. No one wants a coach who is trying to fix them. What's most helpful is someone who believes in them.

Some people make assumptions about themselves at a young age and never recover. At a young age, I made assumptions that just weren't true. I shot for some targets that weren't that important. I've had the benefit of having many great people in my life. They made a difference and encouraged me. You can recover from untrue assumptions, but it is much more productive not to make them in the first place.

Finding your gift is essential, but that discovery will likely not be a straight path. Maybe you are good or bad at something. That doesn't mean you'll reach your potential in that specialty. Reaching one's potential requires hard work and determination. Resiliency is the name of the game when it comes to achievement.

Most of us recognize that we learn more from losing than winning, which is confirmed when trying to find what we are good at. What you end up being good at is not just what comes easier to you. We should never pursue the things that bring us the most comfort in our journey. There are better paths than this.

CHAPTER 20

The Response

There are moments when we either compete or give up. The definition of "compete" can vary depending on the circumstances. Determining the correct one for ourselves is enormously important in our personal and professional lives.

Miriam's Dictionary defines "compete" as "striving consciously or unconsciously for an objective (such as position, profit, or a prize): be in a state of rivalry."[35] Having a child with autism taught me that competing means so much more than this definition. I now see the word "rivalry" as referring to an internal struggle, while external competition is an opportunity for challenge and growth.

Life presents us with lots of choices and opportunities. The trick is learning to respond when challenging moments hit. In those flashes, the skeptic inside of us tells us that we cannot do something. Learning to compete is also about learning to fall forward amongst our fears, planning, preparing, and acting when there is an opportunity and a difficulty.

Theodore Roosevelt, who served as the 26th president of the United States from 1901 to 1909, delivered a speech entitled "Citizens in a Republic" at the Sorbonne in Paris on April 23, 1910. A portion of the address, known as "The Man in the Arena," has become wildly popular:

"It is not the critic who counts, not the man who points out how the strong man stumbles or where the doer of deeds could have done them better. The credit belongs to the man who is actually in the arena, whose face is marred by dust and sweat and blood; who strives valiantly; who errs, who comes short again and again, because there is no effort without error and shortcoming; but who does strive to do the deeds; who knows great enthusiasms, the great devotions; who spends himself in a worthy cause; who at best knows, in the end, the triumph of high achievement, and who at the worst, if he fails, at least fails while daring greatly, so that his place shall never be with those cold and timid souls who neither knows victory nor defeat."[36]

This section of the famous speech is inspiring. Presidents and keynote speakers have often quoted it.

A choice confronts us when we're down, bewildered, and distraught. Are we going to sulk and stay on the sideline, or will we get into the arena and compete? Are we going to get knocked down, get up, and learn?

Elite performance is a lot more than world records and championships. Elite performance is about consistently doing your best every day—and eliminating the excuses that get in the way of being the best version of yourself. Sometimes, it is about getting out of bed, putting the key in the ignition, and pointing your car toward work. Other times, it is about starting that first conversation. Elite performance is not limited to what the outside world sees. Elite performance is dangerous and uncomfortable. Wasting time as a victim isn't an option for an elite performer.

Think briefly about all the single parents. They might be exhausted, broke, isolated, and at the end of their rope. Wouldn't they qualify as elite performers? People with disabilities and special needs compete at an elite level every day. Some of the most courageous people have disabilities. The parents of people with disabilities are often warriors. There's much to learn from the parents of children with special needs. Their life wears them out, but they keep getting into the arena to give their best.

Competing in the game that you're registered for is one way to success. We don't always get to pick the game, so it is pointless to waste time and talent wishing it was a different one. It is easy to think that you should be in another game, but you must win the game you are in. This is true in sports, business, and our personal lives. For example, if you're a tennis player, strive to be the best. Don't waste time wishing you played basketball or soccer. Stephen Stills wrote a song in the '70s that makes much good sense: "Love the One You're With."

CHAPTER 21

Autism

Autism awareness has increased in the last 20 years. According to the CDC, autism currently affects one in 36 kids in the U.S., one in 25 boys, and one in a hundred girls.[37] In 2005, one in 150 children were diagnosed with autism. Earlier recognition and treatment are more readily available, so there's significantly more awareness than ever, but there's a long way to go until the autistic population gets a fair crack.

When Cole was diagnosed, I knew nothing about autism, so I was blindsided when we got the diagnosis. Fear often fills space when we don't know all of the facts. This is one reason it is better to over-communicate than under-communicate. This is true in our relationships with family, management, and leadership. For example, in coaching, the more players know, the more their anxiety level decreases, leading to better team chemistry and performance.

I couldn't prepare for my introduction to autism l because I didn't have prior experience with disabilities or special needs. If I had known more people with autism, my reaction would probably have been different. Awareness is essential. Understanding can also help with acceptance. It isn't the brand of the challenge that's important. It is what can be learned by responding to them. It's important not to waste time being stuck because there is too much fun to be had living with joy, no matter the circumstance.

Cole's journey has been amazing. He's among the most incredible, creative, funny, bright, and courageous people I know. I could not be any prouder. However, my point is that the surprise of the unknown and the fear of broken dreams were the most challenging. As we go through trials, we get stronger. Life doesn't get easier; we get better at adapting. I was devastated when I tore my ACL, but if I tore it again, I would be less upset because now I know what to expect. My experience, although difficult at the time, has given me knowledge about what life afterward could be like.

Experiences equip us to adjust when we run into problems in the future. We talked a lot about pivoting when I was in business school. When entrepreneurs run into roadblocks, they might learn and pivot to a new direction that helps them succeed. We can also pivot in our personal lives so we can go out and do something extraordinary we might not have envisioned. To make the pivot, you must accept that things aren't the same as they were.

This is life training. We train for other things, so why not invest in training for life? There's no other way unless you're settling for second best. You typically learn about humility and resiliency through experience rather than in a class, but if you could learn it in a course, it would be one of the best courses ever taught.

Having an autistic child has taught me a lot about being calm under pressure. Things that mattered before don't matter as much. There are luxuries that I don't have time or energy for anymore. Even tennis matches are less stressful. I've grown a lot in personal strength and fortitude. People sometimes refer to this as "parent strength." This strength comes from trials.

Every day, I spend hours around gifted athletes who spend a lot of time training. They often improve from life experiences more than they do from training. I've become stronger since the initial diagnosis, and it had nothing to do with lifting weights or absorbing protein.

It has been proven repeatedly that we can persevere through much more than we think. It's easy to forget it when the fire is hot. We must note that we can be resilient with belief, determination, and hope.

In the 1950s, a Johns Hopkins professor named Dr. Curt Richter did a study that tested the power of hope. He put rats into a water cylinder to test how long they could swim before drowning. The average rat lasted around 15 minutes before giving up. However, right before the rats sank, Richter would scoop them out and let them rest for a few minutes before putting them back in the same cylinder of water for a second test.

Here's what's so amazing. The second time, the rats would not give up for nearly 60 hours. This time, they believed they would be saved, and that belief allowed them to press on far beyond what the researchers expected. Ultimately, this study proved the significance of hope. "After eliminating hopelessness," wrote Richter, "the rats do not die."[38] If this phenomenon happens with rats, it can happen with us, too. I see this a lot with athletes. Eliminating hopelessness is a game changer. We can't be the best version of ourselves if we're battling despair.

Educating people about hope is an incredible idea. However, when you demonstrate a pattern to yourself of never giving up, you learn more than a class on hope could ever teach you. Examples from stories are helpful, but real hope comes when we recognize challenges as opportunities.

We can turn hopelessness into hopefulness, but it doesn't happen automatically. Hope is based on a combination of facts, faith, and attitude. Attitude is often part of perception or how we see our place in the world. Possessing a great attitude is much easier if you believe you are part of a larger plan. I see this firsthand with the players I coach. Those who play for the team typically have a more upbeat spirit than those who don't.

Despair is the opposite of hope, the state where we don't believe that something good will happen in the future. This is easy to do when you don't understand that your life might be about being helpful to others. You could be part of a bigger plan. This idea is certainly worth exploring.

In *Man's Search for Meaning*, Victor Frankl describes how he stayed alive in a Nazi concentration by searching for and finding meaning in his life. He states, "Suffering ceases to be suffering at the moment it finds meaning." He had to survive because there were things he needed to do that he was uniquely qualified to accomplish. He thought about and dreamed of one day giving lectures. He had a book to write that no one else could, so he needed to survive his imprisonment. He observed that "those who knew there was a task waiting for them to fulfill were most likely to survive." His most significant task was to keep the picture of a future alive.

This is hope. Purpose, meaning, and hope came together in Viktor Frankl's study. In Richter's study, the hope of staying alive got the rats through their ordeal. You and I need hope, too—hope to make a difference and have meaning in our lives. We should all aspire to make a difference and add value to the lives of others. When we do, we might inspire ourselves. This winning spirit should not be limited to sports. We must apply it in family life, our businesses, and everything else we care about.

Individual sports such as tennis are good for teaching perseverance and self-reliance because you can't blame anyone else when you lose. However, you can give away the credit when you win. This is what life is about. Unfortunately, our culture often tries to convince us otherwise, but giving is where we find the most joy. Life is best when played as a team rather than an individual sport. Playing as a team gives us hope. Players on the autism spectrum often play without a team, but it doesn't have to be this way. We can be in the business of giving team membership away and including people in our lives.

Conclusion

We have a God who loves us beyond belief, and he has a fantastic and well-thought-out plan. Fortunately, he hasn't asked me for advice on developing and orchestrating His plan. As far as I can tell, he isn't planning to come to me anytime soon, asking for my assistance with His strategic plan and vision. What makes more sense is that I trust His plan, do my best to understand His wishes, and follow his plan. I can't help but think that high on his list is to help take care of his kids.

Hard Comes First is a love story that describes methods for living well. There's drama, challenge, and fear, but the ending is happy beyond measure. It isn't always easy, but the story is better than ever because of the lessons learned. The tactics and stories are gifts of inspiration that have been given to me that I get to hand off.

Autism awareness has come a long way since my son's diagnosis. However, the numbers continue to rise, as do many challenges that come along with them. The best in life comes when you're fully invested and committed to making a difference in whatever you undertake. The opportunity to help with autism is still full of possibilities and needs, but there are plenty of other areas that require attention as well. Everyone can be a difference maker for something that has a need. Go for it. Life is too short not to make a difference in things beyond ourselves and our desires. This is what purpose is. We have the freedom to choose our purpose and attack it!

Hard Comes First is a road map to a better life, regardless of your story. The point is that our loving God is in control of everything. All we have to do is trust and believe. I wish that I had known this from the beginning. However, if I had, I wouldn't have written this book. This story would have been different, but maybe not as helpful, so who knows, perhaps it worked out just how it was supposed to.

Today, I know that I'm not writing the script. I get to go after life with abundant joy, curiosity, and trust. We have the opportunity to believe that *love* is a verb. In its purest form, love transcends quid pro quo, and it is in this realm that it bestows the most abundant gifts.

Waiting for perfect people to love well isn't a requirement. That is why being a teammate is so great. We don't get to choose our teammates, but we *do* get to choose to love them. Teams aren't limited to sports. Anyone can form a team and love endlessly. Everyone can be a great teammate. Let's go, even if *Hard Comes First.*

THANK YOU FOR READING MY BOOK!

Thank you for reading my book!

Scan the QR Code to Access:

The Accountability Guide to Becoming the Best Version of Yourself

I appreciate your interest in my book and value your feedback as it helps me improve future versions of this book. I would appreciate it if you could leave your invaluable review on Amazon.com with your feedback. Thank you!

References

1. Goleman, Daniel. Emotional Intelligence. Bantam Books

2. https://www.espn.com/sportscentury/athletes.html

3. https://www.ncaa.org/sports/2015/3/2/estimated-probability-of-competing-in-college-Athletics.aspx

4. https://www.wearecollegetennis.com/2022/04/05/pathway-to-the-pros/

5. https://www.marketwatch.com/story/these-are-the-sports-where-foreigners-get-the-most-us-athletic-scholarships-2017-05-11

6. https://www.runnersworld.com/training/a27193782/boston-marathon-winners-age/

7. https://www.hmpgloballearningnetwork.com/site/podiatry/sports-medicine/thirty-years-observations-clubfeet-athletes-and-military

8. https://www.fool.com/the-ascent/credit-cards/articles/the-average-american-has-this-much-credit-card-debt/

9. https://www.pwc.com/gx/en/industries/consumer-markets/consumer-insights-survey.html

10. https://www.hhs.gov/sites/default/files/surgeon-general-social-connection-advisory.pdf

11. https://neurosciencenews.com/autism-loneliness-25149/

12. https://www.ncaa.org/sports/2022/10/14/finances-of-intercollegiate-athletics-division-i-dashboard.aspx

13. https://www.guinnessworldrecords.com/world-records/best-selling-book-of-non-fiction

14. https://www.merriam-webster.com/dictionary/underdog

15. Malcom Gladwell, David, Goliath:Underdogs, Misfits, and the Art of Battling Giants. Published by Little, Brown, and Company

16. https://news.wisc.edu/for-mothers-of-children-with-autism-the-caregiving-life-proves-stressful/

17. Viktor Frankl, Man's Search for Meaning, Beacon Press

18. https://www.today.com/series/things-i-wish-i-knew/things-i-wish-i-d-known-about-having-child-autism-t110323

19. https://www.cdc.gov/ncbddd/disabilityandhealth/infographic-disability-impacts-all.html

20. C.S. Lewis, The Lion, The Witch, and the Wardrobe. Geoffry Bles

21. https://www.health.harvard.edu/blog/what-is-neurodiversity-202111232645

22. https://www.golfdigest.com/courses/sc/kiawah-island-golf-resort-the-ocean-course

23. https://www.espn.com/espn/thelife/news/story?id=5257611

24. https://news.gallup.com/poll/610133/less-half-americans-satisfied-own-lives.aspx

25. https://www.gallup.com/workplace/468233/employee-engagement-needs-rebound-2023.aspx

26. https://hbr.org/2011/11/why-inspiration-matters

27. https://hbr.org/2011/11/why-inspiration-matters

28. https://www.psychologytoday.com/us/blog/the-power-of-prime/200910/sports-what-motivates-athletes

29. Autism Every Day

30. https://www.friendshipcircle.org/blog/2010/11/03/80-divorce-rate-for-parents-with-a-child-who-has-autism#:~:text=Findings%20of%20the%20UW%20study,children%2C%20and%2014%25%20chance%20for

31. https://www.wsj.com/articles/ken-ravizza-pioneered-art-of-coaching-athletes-others-on-thinking-skills-1533911401

32. https://www.autismspeaks.org/news/study-confirms-autism-wandering-common-scary

33. http://www.dbooth.org/guat2000/small/teresa.htm

34. https://www.emilyperlkingsley.com/welcome-to-holland

35. https://www.merriam-webster.com/dictionary/compete

36. https://www.theodorerooseveltcenter.org/Learn-About-TR/TR-Encyclopedia/Culture-and-Society/Man-in-the-Arena.aspx

37. https://www.autismspeaks.org/autism-statistics-asd#:~:text=1%20in%2036%20children%20in,rate%20of%201%20in%2044.&text=In%20the%20U.S.%2C%20about%204,diagnosed%20with%20autism%20than%20girls.

38. https://www.psychologytoday.com/us/blog/kidding-ourselves/201405/the-remarkable-power-hope

Made in the USA
Middletown, DE
17 October 2024

62700737R00102